Effective
Advertising

To
Sonia, whose enthusiasm has been a joy,
Kethan, whose simplicity has been a charm,
Viren, whose enterprise has been an inspiration,
Neil, whose focus has been a model,
Cheryl, whose complete support has been my greatest reward.

Effective Advertising

Understanding When, How, and Why Advertising Works

Gerard J. Tellis

University of Southern California

SAGE Publications
International Educational and Professional Publisher
Thousand Oaks ■ London ■ New Delhi

For information:

Sage Publications, Inc.
2455 Teller Road
Thousand Oaks, California 91320
E-mail: order@sagepub.com

Sage Publications Ltd.
6 Bonhill Street
London EC2A 4PU
United Kingdom

Sage Publications India Pvt. Ltd.
B-42 Panchsheel Enclave
Post Box 4109
New Delhi 110017
India

Printed in the United States of America

Library of Congress Cataloging-in-Publication Data

Tellis, Gerard J., 1950-

Effective advertising: Understanding when, how, and why advertising works / by Gerard J. Tellis.
    p. cm.
Includes bibliographical references and index.
ISBN 0-7619-2252-0 (cloth)—ISBN 0-7619-2253-9 (paper)
   1. Advertising. 2. Consumers-Attitudes. I. Title.
HF5823.T273 2004
659.1—dc22

                       2003016016

03   04   10 9 8 7 6 5 4 3 2 1

Acquiring Editor:	Al Bruckner
Editorial Assistant:	MaryAnn Vail
Production Editor:	Diana E. Axelsen
Copy Editor:	Kate Peterson
Typesetter:	C&M Digitals (P) Ltd.
Indexer:	Jeanne Busemeyer
Cover Designer:	Janet Foulger

Contents

Part I

Understanding Advertising

1

Evaluating Advertising

D oes advertising really work? If yes, when, why, and how does it work? Is it a weak force or a strong force? Is it merely background noise or does it control people's minds? Does it corrupt our societal values or is it an engine of economic growth?

Answers to these questions are critically important because advertising plays an important role in our economy and society. Advertising is a vitally important though much misunderstood force in modern markets. To appreciate the importance of evaluating advertising effectiveness, this chapter first explains the role of advertising in modern markets. The chapter then outlines the complexity of determining the effectiveness of advertising. To understand how advertising works in modern markets, the chapter next explains the key terms used in advertising and the nuances these terms take in this book.

Importance of Advertising in Modern Economies

Advertising is pervasive. Today, advertisers bombard consumers with appeals or reminders from the moment they wake up till the moment they fall asleep. Ads appear on news programs that consumers access, in the entertainment they seek, on billboards as they commute, on Internet sites as they surf the Web, and even in their classrooms and office space. Estimates of the number of ad messages that reach consumers vary from 100 to more than 1,000 a day. Thus, ads greatly impinge on consumers' awareness and have the potential of greatly affecting their thoughts, attitudes, feelings, and decisions.

Many people think that advertising is a lot of hype. They think firms advertise to sell their products to consumers or to make a fast buck. Such people think advertising is an accident of the free economy or an evil that consumers have to endure in the interests of free speech. However, the reality is quite different. Advertising is a vitally important force for several reasons.

First, advertising is a major means of competition among firms.

In a free market, firms constantly compete with each other for sales by offering consumers better quality or lower prices or both. Firms use brand names to represent a consistent level of quality at particular prices. Firms use advertising to communicate to consumers what these brand names represent and at what prices and where they will be available. The various forms of advertising enable firms to communicate with consumers promptly and efficiently as needed. Thus, advertising is essential for the efficient working of competitive markets.

Second, advertising is the primary means by which firms inform consumers about new or improved products.

Over the past couple of centuries, the quality of life of consumers has improved greatly, primarily because of the better goods and services available to consumers. The great vitality of the American economy, indeed of most free market economies, rests on the ability of firms to produce and market these better products to consumers. To do so, firms must be able to communicate with consumers, to inform them of the innovations at hand, and to persuade them of the value of these innovations. Advertising has emerged as the primary means by which firms achieve this task. Thus, advertising has the potential to ensure the vital functioning of markets for new and improved products.

Third, advertising provides major support for the media in the United States and many other countries.

Several media, including broadcast TV, much of cable TV, newspapers, magazines, and much of the Internet, reach consumers either free or much below cost. The reason is that advertisers pay media owners for displaying their ads. Media owners in turn do not have to charge consumers the full cost of the media. As such, advertising subsidizes these media. The media themselves are an important means of information and entertainment for consumers. Thus, advertising subsidizes the free flow of information and entertainment to consumers.

Fourth, advertising is a huge industry.

Total expenditures on all media advertising (excluding mail and telephone), in 2002, were more than $236 billion.[1] The industry involves more than 21,000 firms and employed 302,000 people in 2000.[2] In the first decade of this century, employment in the advertising industry is likely to grow 32%, compared with 15% on average for all industries.[3]

Fifth, the public subsidizes advertising expenditures.

Advertising expenditures in the United States and many capitalist countries are tax deductible. That is, firms can charge these expenditures as costs of doing business to lower their pretax profits. In effect, the public pays for a fraction of the cost of advertising that is equal to the advertiser's marginal tax rate. More generally, assuming a positive tax rate, the public subsidizes a portion of advertising expenditures.

SUMMARY

All these factors suggest that several groups have a vital interest in knowing how advertising works. These groups include advertisers, ad agencies, public policy makers, consumers, and voters. Advertisers themselves need to know how it works in order to achieve their advertising goals and make the best use of their resources. Ad agencies that plan, evaluate, and implement ad campaigns need to know how advertising works in order to be more efficient stewards of their clients' resources. Public policy makers need to know how advertising works in order to regulate advertising in the public interest. Consumers need to know how advertising works in order to best interpret ads and make good purchase decisions. Voters need to know how advertising works in order to understand the value of the public subsidy of advertising.

Problems Evaluating Advertising Effectiveness

Despite its importance and wide implications, evaluating the effectiveness of advertising is very difficult. The difficulty occurs because advertising's working is highly complex. It depends intrinsically on human response to communication. Thus, it involves complexities in the attention, processing, recall, and response to the appeal. To begin to realize how complex this issue is, consider the following problems in evaluating how an ad for a brand can affect a consumer's purchase of that brand.

First, consumers may buy a product for a variety of reasons. These reasons include seeing an ad for the brand, satisfaction with the product from past purchases, word-of-mouth recommendations from other consumers, change of taste, prestige attached to the product, an attractive package, a store display, a sales promotion, or an attractive price. Advertising is only one of the many causes that prompt a user to buy a brand. Thus, analyzing what effect the ad has on purchase requires the analyst to fully understand and control the effect of all these other factors.

Second, advertising for a brand may occur in different media. Each of these media may have a unique effect on consumers. To fully understand the role of advertising, the analyst must decode the partial effects of the ad in each of these media. Also, when media overlap, their effects interact, requiring further disentangling.

Third, advertising may have not only instantaneous effects but also carryover effects. An instantaneous effect occurs when a consumer sees an ad and responds to it immediately (see Exhibit 1.1A). For example, an ad for a new kitchen knife set may include an 800 number. On seeing this ad, a viewer might dial the number instantly to buy the product. However, in many cases, consumers do not respond instantaneously to ads but after a period of waiting to think about the ad, talk to friends, do some more research, or buy at an opportune moment. This delay in the effect of an ad is called the *carryover* (see Exhibit 1.1B for one type of carryover). Chapter 7 discusses this phenomenon in depth. So one has to determine how the effect of any single ad decays over the period following its exposure.

Fourth, the effectiveness of the ad may also vary over the life of a campaign. Advertisers normally resort to repetitive advertising. They keep using an ad or a campaign for several days, weeks, or months. The effect of any single ad exposure decays over a period of time as indicated above. However, the effect of each ad may change over the life of the campaign: *Wearin* is an initial increase in the effect of one ad, with repetition during a campaign, because of consumers' increasing familiarity with the ad. *Wearout* is the ultimate decline over time because of consumers' increasing tedium with the ad (see Exhibit 1.2). If the effectiveness of advertising is itself changing over time, determining its effectiveness becomes more complex, because one has to analyze the full impact of a moving target.

Fifth, successive ads have overlapping effects and overlapping decays. If one combines the last three effects described above (wearin, wearout, and carryover), one gets overlapping decays of multiple exposures of an ad, each of which may have different levels of response. Each ad exposure may have a different effect due to consumers' familiarity or tedium. Furthermore, the carryover of one ad exposure adds to or overlaps with the carryover of a prior ad exposure. This overlap in effectiveness creates a new level of complexity in analyzing advertising's effectiveness (see Exhibit 1.2).

Finally, advertising response varies by segments and individuals within a market. A market can be segmented by groups of consumers, each with a similar response to a brand. Some could be loyal users, others, light users, still others, aware but not users, and still others, not even aware of the

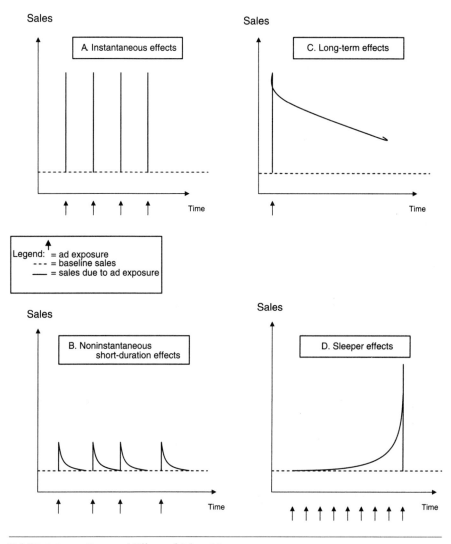

Exhibit 1.1   Temporal Effects of Advertising

brand. Each of these different segments may respond differently to an ad. So when one analyzes ad effectiveness, one has to take into account these different segments to fully understand the phenomenon. If one does not have detailed data, the problem is intractable. But even if one has detailed data, the problem is quite complex, because one has to analyze the effects on these different segments and pool them together to arrive at an overall effect.

The analysis of advertising's effects can be broken down into three important steps or stages:

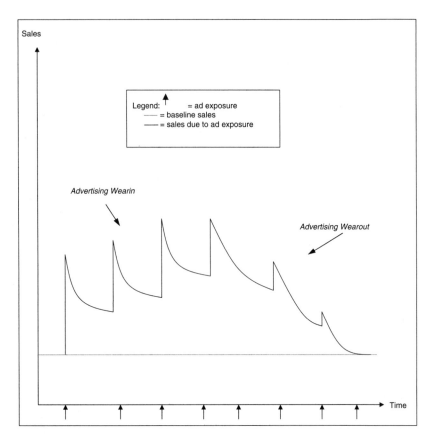

Exhibit 1.2   Wearin and Wearout in Advertising Effectiveness

- Key measures of advertising
- Research designs to evaluate advertising's effects
- Models to relate the variables and measure the effects of advertising

Chapter 4 explains the measures of advertising, and Chapter 5 explains the evaluation of advertising's effects. The next chapter, 2, summarizes common myths about advertising effectiveness in contrast to the major findings from research. The subsequent chapter, 3, presents a general theory of advertising that summarizes and integrates the contents of the other chapters. Chapters 6 and 7 describe the major market findings about advertising's effects. Chapters 8 to 11 describe the major findings about which *creative* is effective and why it is effective. (The term *creative* refers to all design aspects of an ad such as copy, visual and sound aspects, appeal, endorsers, etc.)

Explanation of Key Terms

To explain the broad scope of advertising without getting into a multiplicity of terms, this book uses eight simple terms in a very broad or generic sense that encompasses a variety of contexts in which advertising occurs. This use of the terms may differ from that typically associated with their common use. So this section explains the meaning of the following eight terms: advertising, firm, consumer, product, brand, purchase, advertiser, and market effects.

Advertising is any paid message that a firm delivers to consumers in order to make its offer more attractive to them. The term *firm* means any person or organization of any size that has something to offer another. Similarly, the term *consumer* means any person or organization that is the target of a firm's offer. The term *product* means any good, service, idea, or person that an organization wants to offer to a consumer. Examples of a firm-product-consumer triad include the following:

- Soap-maker marketing soap to households
- Automaker marketing cars to car rental companies
- Gardener marketing a day's labor to a homeowner
- Manufacturer recruiting fresh graduates
- Law firm marketing legal services to plaintiffs
- Politician marketing candidacy to voters
- Church marketing inner renewal to believers

The term *brand* means a clearly distinguishable name, which a firm uses to uniquely identify its product with consumers and distinguish it from that of competitors. For example, Cathedral of Our Lady of the Angels is the brand name of the newly opened Catholic cathedral in Los Angeles. In an attempt to exploit the equity in its brand, in its gift shop, the cathedral sells its own wine, branded Cathedral of Our Lady of the Angels Chardonnay.[4] The term *purchase* means the key behavior of a consumer desired by the firm. In the examples above, the term purchase could mean a believer attending services in the cathedral, a household buying soap, a citizen voting for a candidate, or a plaintiff signing on a law firm as its legal representative. Thus, purchase refers to activities such as buying a car, voting for a candidate, hiring an employee, or praying in a church. We refer to firms that advertise to consumers as the *advertiser*.

Soap and food are traditional markets where advertising has been used effectively for centuries. For example, one of the first national ad campaigns was Procter & Gamble's successful advertising of Ivory soap in the 1870s that made it a national brand.[5] Indeed, the science of advertising probably developed earliest from its use in these markets. However, advertising can be used as well in nontraditional markets such as seeking jobs, soliciting clients, canvassing for votes, or recruiting worshippers. While the book uses a traditional set of terms, it implies a fairly broad domain of application.

As Chapter 4 shows, advertising can have an impact on various mental processes of consumers. However, in the final analysis, for most firms, the value of advertising depends on what effects it has on purchase. For this reason, I define the *market effects* of advertising narrowly to mean any measurable impact of advertising on purchase. The effects of advertising on mental processes are also valid topics of inquiry that help to understand why an ad works or does not work and how it should be redesigned.

Notes

1. Coen, Robert (2003), *Insider Report,* June, NY: Universal McCann (McCann-Erickson WorldGroup).

2. See http://www.bls.gov/oco/cg/cgs030.htm.

3. Ibid.

4. Lopez, Steve (2002), "Parking Fee May Pave Way to Forgiveness, Even Heaven," *Los Angeles Times,* August 30, B1.

5. Tellis, Gerard J. (1998), *Advertising and Sales Promotion Strategy,* Reading, MA: Addison-Wesley.

2

Sweet, Secret
Workings of Advertising

Despite decades of research on advertising, myths abound about its effectiveness. Many of these myths are firmly held by consumers or the public at large, even though a little self-reflection might undermine confidence in them. Many people have naïve beliefs about how advertising affects (other) people in general, though they would reject those same beliefs about themselves. In general, because advertising is pervasive and lies within the common experience of consumers, most people believe that they have a reasonable opinion about how it works.

Even advertising professionals may hold on to some myths about advertising. This happens because of their reliance solely on personal experience, their personal attribution of how advertising works, or their resort to armchair theorizing.

Here are some of the most common myths about advertising effectiveness. Not every one believes in every proposition on this list. Actually, some of these propositions directly contradict others. But many people hold on to one or the other of these propositions in isolation of the others.

Myths About Advertising Effectiveness

Advertising is a powerful force in contemporary markets.

Many people believe that most or all advertising is a powerful force that shapes competition in markets today. This belief probably arises from the pervasiveness of advertising and the huge sums that firms spend on advertising. It seems reasonable to conclude that firms would not spend all that money if advertising were not very effective. The belief in advertising may also arise from famous stories of creative advertising that launched successful new products (e.g., the Windows 95 introductory ad campaign) or highly creative advertising that popularized some brand names (e.g., Intel inside, DeBeers, Marlboro cigarettes). From such famous but rare examples many conclude that advertising is a powerful force. Casual observation also supports the power of advertising in that the heaviest advertising is by brands with the largest market share or highest prices. From that superficial correlation, people conclude that advertising enables firms to have high market share or high prices. These observations and stories feed the erroneous belief that advertising is a powerful force.

Advertising creates consumer needs.

Many people believe that advertising creates consumer needs. This belief is a corollary of the previous one, though it may also arise from casual observation. Many consumers desire or even crave products that are also heavily advertised. Examples are appealing dinners at expensive restaurants, fancy holiday cruises, luxurious sports cars, or stylish clothes. Consumers may learn of these product or brand names from advertising. Consumers may buy products they notice in ads or they may see other consumers using products, which they themselves yearn to possess. All these casual observations may lead them to conclude that those who buy or use the products are doing so as a result of advertising. Thus, people are prone to conclude that advertising creates needs by strongly influencing their minds and desires.[1]

Advertising's effects persist for decades.

Both consumers and advertisers might believe that the effects of advertising last for decades. This belief arises from the casual observation that we are able to remember some very old slogans. Another common observation is that some long-surviving brands have been heavy and consistent advertisers. These two observations seem to support the conclusion that consistent advertising over an extended period of time is responsible for the long-term success of brands.

Even if advertising does not work now, repetition will ensure ultimate success.

Many advertisers like to believe that even if their ads do not work now, they will ultimately do so if repeated long enough. This premise starts with the reasonable assumption that advertising is unlikely to be *fully* effective on the very first exposure. Consumers need to see an ad several times, think about it, and discuss it with friends before being persuaded by it. Moreover, even then, consumers may have to wait for the appropriate time to buy the advertised product. Thus, advertising may have carryover effects, which are visible in periods following exposure to the ad.

From this reasonable assumption, some advertisers may leap to the conclusion that even if an ad *is entirely ineffective now,* time and repetition will ensure its ultimate success. Another way of stating the same premise is that advertising takes a long time to wear in with consumers. From this reasoning arises the recommendation that even if advertising seems ineffective initially, persistence with the campaign will ultimately bear fruit.

One to three exposures are enough for effective advertising.

In contrast to the prior premise, some analysts believe that very few exposures are enough for effective advertising. A General Electric researcher, Herbert Krugman, first started a debate on this issue with his thesis that "three exposures may be enough" for advertising to be effective.[2] Krugman suggested that the first ad would draw attention to a brand, the second would stimulate liking for the brand, and the third would persuade a consumer to buy the brand. This reasoning definitely covers some of the key stages that many consumers go through on the way to making a purchase. It also has a certain intuitive appeal and relies on a favorite magic number, 3. A few well-known studies also conclude that a small number of ad exposures achieve optimal effectiveness. For example, in the 1970s, one advertising researcher, Colin McDonald, found that advertising response peaked at two exposures. Recently, an advertising professor, John Philip Jones, argued that one exposure per week was enough for effective advertising.[3] Thus, belief in a small "right" number of ad exposures has persisted, even though the premise lacks strong theoretical foundation or wide empirical support.

Ironically, this premise runs counter to the previous one or the next one. Yet people may hold on to these views without seeing the inherent contradiction.

Firms often use subliminal advertising.

The term *subliminal* means without being explicitly perceived by the audience. James Vicary, a private market researcher, claimed to have shown, with an experiment he ran in 1957, that subliminal advertising works.[4] His study has never been replicated and is now believed to be fictitious. However, publicity about his study, in the press and in books, has led to a pervasive belief by the public in the efficacy of subliminal advertising. Due to this belief, the Federal Trade Commission outlawed this form of advertising in 1974.[5] The public's belief is probably fed by its suspicion of big business and big advertising.

The belief may also be supported by the public's lack of understanding of how contemporary advertising works, especially when so many of the ads say nothing new or substantive. Thus, many people come to the conclusion that advertising works subliminally. By that term, consumers probably mean that advertising works in some subconscious or subtle way.

Humor in advertising trivializes the message.

Humor in advertising is very common. Often, the humor is weakly related or even unrelated to the brand. Such ads may seem to trivialize the brand or message. While people enjoy such ads, they often wonder what goal they serve and whether they are at all effective. Even some professionals question the role of humor. For example, Claude Hopkins, "a grandfather of modern advertising, asserted that 'frivolity has no place in advertising.'"[6]

Sex sells.

Ads based on sex appeal generally draw the attention of audiences. Some ads are so provocative as to trigger severe criticism in the press and outrage among some segments of the population. For example, in the 2003 Super Bowl, Miller Lite aired a commercial showing two scantily clad women in a catfight about the taste and lightness of the beer. Miller attempted sequels to the ad, even though it won awards for the worst ads of the year and was severely critiqued by reporters. The frequency and persistence of sex appeals in advertising and the attention that such ads get from audiences and reporters, either positive or negative, have led many people to believe "Sex sells." Some go as far to say that it is a powerful force that corrupts our perceptions and lifestyles.[7]

The most effective ad appeal is clear information with strong arguments.

In contrast to the previous belief, many consumers believe that frivolous or "subliminal" advertising is ineffective; the only ads that work are those that embody arguments. This belief relies on the assumption that most consumers make decisions based on the comparative performance of rival brands on specific characteristics. Even if consumers buy a brand due to loyalty or some intangible feeling, they may attribute their purchase to the superiority of the chosen brand over the rival on some attribute. They are reassured with advertising that emphasizes the merits of the brand they use on those attributes. Furthermore, they think that such information clearly points out the appropriate brand to other consumers. From this reasoning, they conclude that the most effective advertising is that which provides clear information about brand attributes on key characteristics. Many copywriters mirror this belief by assuming that they must engage consumers into an active processing of the ad for it to be effective.[8]

The best creatives arise from uniqueness.

The term *creatives* refers to the composite of the content and artistic components of an ad. A major task of advertisers is to develop creatives that grab consumers' attention, incorporate the message succinctly, and persuade consumers of the message. Of these goals, advertisers today seem to put an inordinate amount of importance on grabbing attention.[9] Also, there is a persistent belief among creative artists that the route to grab attention with eye-stopping ads is to be absolutely unique or entirely different from prevailing ads. Thus, the golden rule seems to be "Be unique." This belief rests on the assumption that creativity cannot be programmed, defined by rules, or informed by templates. Rather, it arises from illogical, divergent, or "lateral" thinking or thinking "out of the box."

Advertising is very profitable.

One of the most common beliefs of the public is that advertising is very profitable. The public suspects that big advertising involves large sums of money. Indeed, many large firms invest huge sums of money on advertising, year after year. People who observe such advertising are prone to conclude that firms would not do so if that advertising did not bring in great profits. Also, some of the largest and most profitable brands are also big spenders in advertising. From these two observations, it is easy for them to conclude that advertising is very profitable.

Truth About Advertising

Extensive review of more than 50 years of rigorous research on advertising suggests some important conclusions about its effects on sales. These conclusions can be grouped into four classes: effects of advertising intensity, advertising dynamics, advertising strategy, and advertising contingencies. Here I briefly explain some important conclusions, under these topics. Detailed explanations and support for these conclusions are available in the rest of the book. In particular, Chapters 6 and 7 document the support for most of these hypotheses.

EFFECTS OF ADVERTISING INTENSITY

Advertising intensity or weight refers to the level of advertising. Because the development of an ad takes time, in the short term, managers often modify advertising strategy by increasing or decreasing the weight or intensity of advertising. What effects do such changes have on sales? Decades of research have led to potential generalizations about consumer and market response to changes in advertising intensity. Chapter 6 covers these effects in depth with detailed references for supporting research. This section merely summarizes the main findings.

Weight alone is not enough.

To wring additional sales from an ad campaign, firms often resort to increases in advertising weight. Sometimes these increases can be quite large, on the order of 100% or even 200%. Numerous studies have shown that mere increases in advertising weight do not yield dramatic or sometimes even *any* changes in sales. Similarly, decreases and even cessation in advertising do not lead to an immediate decrease in sales. Changes in other aspects of advertising do lead to increase in sales (see the last two subsections in this chapter); thus, the conclusion, "Weight alone is not enough." The moral behind these findings is that many firms in mature industries are probably advertising at the market's saturation point or they are overadvertising.[10] Chapter 6 details support for these conclusions.

Advertising is a subtle force.

Closely related to this point are the effects of advertising when change in intensity does matter. The effects of changes in ad intensity can be measured in terms of its elasticity. The *elasticity of sales to advertising*, also called *advertising elasticity*, is the percentage change in sales for a 1% change in advertising. This is the simplest measure of the effectiveness of advertising. Over the past 50 years, several researchers have estimated the advertising elasticity across a variety of categories, countries, types of data, stages of the product life cycle, and types of statistical models. To get a sense of any potential generalizations in this area, a few authors have carried out summaries of the findings from these studies. One such summary found that on average the advertising elasticity is significantly different from 0, but is only .1.[11] This number means that if the advertising budget increases by 1%, sales would increase by only .1%.[12] This small number means that advertising is not generally the powerful force in moving consumers to act as many people think it is. Rather, it is a subtle force that must be skillfully planned and carefully deployed to maximize its effectiveness. A few ad campaigns do have dramatic effects, as explained below.

For example, the advertising elasticity of Absolut's advertising is similar to the average given above. Yet consistent advertising for Absolut over a 20-year period in the United States *gradually* moved it from an inconsequential brand with less than 1% share in 1981 to the second largest vodka brand with about a 12% share in 2000.[13] In retrospect, the change in share is enormous. In practice, it occurred over a long period of time, with a massive level of advertising. Thus, the advertising elasticity is quite small.

In contrast to advertising, the effects of changes in price are clearly evident and generally strong. The strength or effectiveness of pricing can also be compared in terms of its elasticity. Analogous to advertising elasticity, *price elasticity* is the percentage change in sales for a 1% change in price.

Just as for advertising, researchers have conducted a large number of studies to estimate price elasticity. A review and summary of those studies find that price elasticity is on average −1.7.[14] This number means that if price declines by 1%, sales would increase by 2%. Recall that advertising elasticity is .1. Note that the two elasticities have opposite signs. This means that price increases cause sales *decreases,* and advertising increases cause sales *increases.*

What's more important is the big difference in the magnitude of the two elasticities. Price elasticity is more than 15 times greater than advertising elasticity in absolute value. In other words, the same *percentage* change in price or the advertising budget will yield dramatically different percentage changes in sales. The sales response for price changes will be 15 times stronger (although in the opposite direction) than that for advertising changes. Chapter 6 summarizes the studies that led to these conclusions.

However, high price elasticity comes at a steep cost—discounts in price or a strategy of everyday low prices. Either strategy can hurt the bottom line, profits. In contrast, subtle responsiveness to advertising comes at a potentially big gain—increases in sales or price with potentially small increases in costs.

Subtle does not mean ineffective. Subtle means small changes that have to be carefully exploited over an extended period of time.

The effects of advertising are fragile.

The term *fragile* means that the effect is easily lost or biased by the use of the wrong analysis or method. The researcher has to analyze data carefully with appropriate methods to observe the correct effect of advertising. The effects of advertising are fragile for three reasons. First, the effects of advertising are relatively subtle especially when compared to the effects of price or promotion. Second, the effects of advertising are not *entirely* instantaneous. *Some* of the effects of advertising occur over time and must be carefully analyzed. For example, the State of California's aggressive antismoking campaign may have caused a shift in youth attitudes away from cigarette smoking. But the change did not occur overnight. Third, the effects of advertising are easily biased. The bias may occur for several reasons. If advertising occurs at the same time as sales promotions, failure to properly control for sale promotions may cause advertising to wrongly appear stronger than it really is. Advertising may also appear to be strongly related to sales because managers set advertising levels in expectation of certain sales, rather than because advertising causes sales. In addition, the use of aggregate data (such as quarterly or annual figures) tends to upwardly bias the effects of ads if the latter were scheduled on a daily or weekly basis. Chapter 5 explains how research can carefully estimate these fragile effects of advertising.

Firms often persist with ineffective ads.

At face value, this seems like a self-contradictory premise. Why would firms indulge in ineffective advertising? There are several reasons for their behavior. Most important, many firms do not regularly and routinely test the effectiveness of their advertising. Rather, they invest in advertising based on historical patterns or competitive pressure. Second, the effects of advertising are fragile and difficult for firms to estimate or observe. Thus, risk-averse firms tend to invest in advertising even if they are not sure it works, rather than not invest and see the demise of their brands. Third, competition pressurizes firms to overadvertise. Fourth, the reward system within firms may be based on sales rather than on profits after taking into account the costs of ads. If so, managers are prone to advertise even if that advertising is unprofitable, so long as it holds out the hope of increased sales. Fifth, the annual budgeting system within firms may encourage managers to spend their budget on advertising early on, rather than to hold on to it until year end when they face budget cuts. Sixth, many firms rely on advertising agencies for both the development and deployment of ad campaigns and the evaluation of those campaigns. Also, sometimes agencies are compensated on a fraction of the advertising budget they recommend for their clients. In either of these cases, conflict of interests between what's good for the agencies (heavy advertising) and what's good for the firm (prudent advertising) may hinder wise decisions, such as a cutback of ineffective advertising. Chapter 3 covers this issue in greater depth.

Advertising may be often unprofitable.

Research indicates that firms tend to overadvertise. Such behavior occurs because of the use of ineffective ads or the continuation of an ad campaign that has ceased to be effective. However, advertisers have to pay the media whether or not their advertising is effective. This situation may result in the continuation of unprofitable advertising.

DYNAMIC EFFECTS OF ADVERTISING

Chapter 7 discusses all these dynamic effects in depth. Here I merely summarize the main findings.

Advertising's effects are not instantaneous.

Exhibit 1.1A in Chapter 1 shows such an instantaneous effect. In this graph, time is plotted along the horizontal axis and sales along the vertical axis. The dotted line is the baseline sales, and the solid line is the effect of advertising on sales. The short arrow indicates the occurrence of an advertising exposure.

The effects of advertising are not entirely instantaneous. *Some* portion of the effect of advertising carries over to periods following exposure to the ad, for several reasons. First, consumers take time to think about the ads and be convinced about its message. Second, some consumers might be convinced only after discussing the message with other consumers, while still others may get the message only secondhand from consumers who saw the ad. Third, even when convinced, consumers may not make a purchase until they are out of stock or feel the need for the product. For all of these reasons, some of the effects of advertising may carry over beyond the period of exposure. Chapter 7 reviews the findings on this point.

Because of these carryover effects, advertisers can stop advertising for brief periods of time without suffering immediate loss in sales. Indeed, when unaware of these carryover effects, advertisers may overuse an effective campaign. Scheduling of advertising in flights, with temporary suspension between flights, may be more effective and efficient than continuous advertising at an even rate year-round.

Advertising carryover is generally short.

Many people including some researchers believe that the effects of advertising last a very long time, years or even decades. Exhibit 1.1C in Chapter 1 shows such an effect. Here time may be measured in months or years. The effect of any one ad or ad campaign is shown to last for many such periods.

The belief that advertising effects last for years or decades arises from two sources. First, some formal but very old studies, using aggregate[15] annual data, showed that carryover effects of advertising lasted an average of four to five years. However, subsequent studies showed quite convincingly that the carryover effect in years was due to the use of annual data. When researchers used disaggregate[16] data in weeks, days, or hours, they estimated carryover effects to last weeks, days, or hours, respectively. (Chapter 7 discusses this issue and the problems with aggregate and disaggregate data in greater detail.)

Second, on reflection, we often easily remember slogans, ads, and themes of certain well-advertised brands many years after they started or stopped. However, the ability to recall ads or advertised slogans does not automatically mean people will buy the advertised brands. For example, many people remember AT&T's ad tagline "Reach out and touch someone." But AT&T is still in serious competitive trouble, and few people choose the service today because of that great memorable slogan. Similarly, many people remember the ad tagline "When E. F. Hutton talks people listen." No matter, the firm is dead.

For most advertising, effects last only a short time because of the noise from competing ads, consumers' poor attention to ads, and the competition for consumers' memory from newer messages that are constantly being advertised. Chapter 7 discusses these issues in greater depth. Exhibit 1.1B shows this pattern of response to advertising. Time here could be in weeks or even days.

Advertising is effective either early on or never.

In the face of weak or no response to some ad campaigns, managers may believe that they need to give the campaign more time to work. They may reason that advertising works in the long run through repetition. This belief implies that advertising works through some subconscious or unconscious mechanism and needs time to "work" itself into an audience's consciousness. Such an effect may also be called a sleeper effect. Exhibit 1.1D shows this effect graphically.

In fact, research indicates that mere repetition of an *ineffective* ad campaign does not make it effective.[17] If one does not see any results early on (such as in the first few weeks of repetition), the campaign will probably be ineffective in the long run too. Chapter 7 details this issue.

EFFECTS OF AD CAMPAIGNS

The term *ad campaign* here refers to a schedule of appearances of the same ad over a period of time.

Successes can be dramatic, although rare.

A dramatic success is one in which advertising achieves a huge increase or reversal in the performance of a brand in a short period of time—a few months to a year. Advertising, especially in free markets, occurs in the context of aggressive competition. In this context, dramatic successes are rare for several reasons. First, the noise level from competing ads is very high. It creates a huge barrier, above which a new ad needs to rise just to be heard. Second, firms are in a constant struggle to come up with creative ads and with winning campaigns. Competition among firms ensures that all well-known appeals and creative platforms have already been used and probably overused. Third, human limitations render it tough for creative artists to make every ad campaign a dramatic success. Finally, whenever a firm does create a winning campaign, competitors quickly imitate the appeal and compete away its effectiveness. Viewed differently, it is not that the technology does not exist for highly effective advertising. Rather, it is competition among firms that neutralizes the effectiveness of a winning creative.

For example, after the success of Apple's "1984" ad aired during the Super Bowl, TV commercials increasingly resorted to drama to introduce new products during the Super Bowl. Prices for advertising during the Super Bowl kept increasing, until they reached a peak of $2.3 million for 30 seconds in 2000. However, examples of dramatic success such as the 1984 ad are rare. Chapter 3 discusses this premise.

Wearin is very rapid, while wearout occurs early.

An ad in a campaign has a sales response curve with respect to characteristics such as size, appeal, or execution. Let us assume that the ad's designer has chosen the optimum size, appeal, and execution. Now, that optimal response itself varies over the life of the campaign. In the first few weeks of the campaign, the effectiveness of the ad may increase as consumers pay more attention to it and understand it better. This increase in effectiveness is called *wearin*. However, with repetition, its effectiveness may plateau and then even decline, due to consumers' increasing tedium with the campaign. The decreasing effectiveness of the ad over time is called *wearout*. Exhibit 1.2 in Chapter 1 shows this response graphically.

Research shows that the wearin of an ad in a campaign is quite rapid and may sometimes not even occur. That is, ads reach their peak effectiveness almost immediately from the start of the campaign. This premise is consistent with a prior finding that ads are effective either early on or never.[18] Thus, a sleeper effect is highly unlikely. An ad in a campaign may wear in more slowly if it occurs in the field, is scheduled infrequently, uses an emotional appeal, or targets consumers who are not active processors of the ads.

In contrast, ads tend to wear out relatively rapidly, perhaps in 6 to 12 weeks. In other words, after 6 to 12 weeks, an ad in a campaign is not as effective as when the campaign was initially introduced and may not be effective at all. Then it is time for a new ad. Continuation of the old ad by further repetition would be unproductive. Wearout may occur more slowly if an ad is complex, uses an emotional appeal, or the exposures are scheduled apart. Campaigns that use a variety of creative executions delay the wearout because the variety delays the onset of tedium. Chapter 7 summarizes the evidence in support of these premises.

Hysterisis is very rare.

The term *hysterisis* means that the effects of a campaign on sales hold even when the campaign is suspended. For instance, one of the most successful ads ever is Apple's "1984" ad during the Super Bowl that year to launch its Macintosh computers. In an echo of George Orwell's novel *1984*, the ad depicts Big Brother (i.e., IBM) lecturing the faithful through a giant screen in an auditorium. A young woman athlete comes running down the gangway with a sledgehammer and hurls it at the screen, smashing it to bits. The tagline read, "In 1984 Apple introduces the Macintosh. And 1984 will not be like *1984*" of Orwell's novel.

The ad was universally praised by critics and widely covered by the press. The ad was aired only once, but because of its novel use of drama, it received extensive replay in the press. The ad was credited with influencing sales of 72,000 units in the first day, 50% over target.[19] Moreover, sales of the Macintosh continued to soar and contributed to a hugely successful introduction of the product.

Although very rare, this continued effect even after the ad is suspended could occur for one or more of the following reasons. The advertised product is much superior to competitors' due to some innovation. The ad campaign itself uses a novel and effective appeal, medium, or message. The ad gets extensive replay from the press. Once consumers learn of the new product, they continue to buy or repurchase the product and create positive word-of-mouth about it even in the absence of advertising. Thus, the initial advertising merely seeds the word about the innovative product. Chapter 7 reviews the few studies in support of hysterisis.

EFFECTS OF ADVERTISING CREATIVE

Novelty is key to effective advertising.

The bane of advertising is excessive repetition of the same tired ad or message. Faced with weak effects, managers are prone to increase the intensity or level of advertising. But, as pointed out above, this strategy is often futile. Rather, novelty in message, media, target segment, product, and especially creative is more likely to lead to increases in sales than is a mere increase in ad intensity. Chapters 6 and 7 review the studies that support this premise.

This premise about novelty is consistent with the earlier ones that suggest that firms generally advertise at or past the point of saturation. In that case, increases in the level of advertising are unlikely to do much good. The saturation, at least partly if not mostly, emerges from consumers' tedium with the current form of advertising. So a change in any aspect of advertising injects novelty that overcomes the tedium, rejuvenates the advertising, and increases its effectiveness.

For example, to launch its urgent mail service, FedEx (formerly Federal Express) developed its memorable and expressive slogan "When it absolutely, positively has to be there overnight." It repeated the slogan through very heavy advertising. To retain the freshness of its advertising and show the importance of the service in different environments, FedEx developed a large number of ads that reiterated the same tagline. The best known in the set included the fast-talking Mr. Spleen, who exemplified the fast-pace world we live in and thus the need for a fast, reliable service. The campaign, together with the unique service, propelled FedEx as the leader of urgent mail delivery service in the world.

Emotion may be the most effective ad appeal.

Ads can adopt a variety of appeals. The three most common are arguments, emotions, and endorsements. Chapters 9, 10, and 11 explain these three types of appeals in depth. Here we consider a brief definition and summary of the main conclusions of their relative effectiveness.

Arguments are appeals that persuade by use of evidence or force of logic. An emotional appeal is one that persuades by arousing the *emotions*. The message is typically embedded in a drama with a plot played out by characters. The plot engages a subject, leads him or her to identify with the characters, and accept the message. *Endorsements* involve use of a lay endorser, a celebrity, or an expert who vouches for the effectiveness of the product, explicitly by a claim or implicitly by association.

Of the variety of appeals, emotional appeals are probably the most effective for several reasons. First, emotional appeals are more interesting and can more easily cut through the clutter and grab consumers' attention than do other types of appeals. Second, emotional appeals require less concentration on the part of consumers than other types of appeals. Third, emotional appeals are more vivid and better remembered than other types of appeals. Fourth, emotional appeals lead to less counterarguments and thus less resistance from consumers than do other types of appeals. Fifth, emotional appeals lead more immediately to action that any other appeals.

For example, one of the reasons that Nike's ads have been so successful is that they aroused emotions for a mundane product, shoes, which was previously advertised typically through information or endorsements. Nike's ads aroused a variety of emotions, including pride, self-empowerment, determination, and valor, to create a distinct image for its brand and successfully persuade consumers.[20]

Humor works.

Humor in advertising can work for several reasons. First, humor relaxes an audience, making the audience receptive to a message. Second, humor distracts an audience from counterarguing. Third, humor can help to attract an audience and retain attention to the ad—humor leaves an audience in a positive disposition, which can transfer over to the brand. A special strength of humor is that it can be included in any creative and combined with any other form of persuasion. Moreover, humor does not take much time or place. Rather, its effectiveness increases with brevity. Chapter 10 discusses the role of humor in greater depth.

Firms rarely if ever use subliminal advertising.

Most modern research has failed to replicate the findings of subliminal advertising that Vicary achieved in the 1950s. Indeed, he himself supposedly disappeared after making a lot of money in a short period of time, with the claim of effective subliminal advertising. Current theory strongly disputes the effectiveness of subliminal advertising. The logic is the following: If overt advertising that is perceived by consumers itself is weakly effective, then that which is not perceived is unlikely to have any effect. As such, subliminal advertising is neither typically used by firms nor recommended by analysts and consultants. If it were, it would be the panacea to cure all personal and social ills, such as addiction, violence, and so forth.[21] Chapter 8 briefly covers the history and thinking on subliminal advertising.

Templates can foster creativity.

Research indicates that being "different" is neither the only nor sufficient key to effective creatives. On the contrary, effective creatives can emerge from templates.[22] Moreover, the use of creatives can lead to even more effective ads than the reliance on simple norms or rules such as be different; use lateral, divergent, or illogical thinking; or think out of the box. The basis for such templates is the scientific learning that has accumulated over the past 100 years. Such research has analyzed the problems in persuasion and the methods of solving these problems from numerous dimensions. The findings are not always obvious. Moreover, persuasion itself is a highly complex phenomenon. Indeed, Chapters 8, 9, 10, and 11 review these findings and discuss how they can be incorporated into effective advertising.

CONTINGENT EFFECTS OF ADVERTISING

The term *contingent* means depending on contexts or environments. The effects of advertising differ over various contexts. Some of the most important contingent effects deal with novelty in the product, positioning, message, medium or target segments, the level of consumer loyalty, or the type of appeal.[23]

Advertising is more effective for new than mature products.

There could be three reasons for the conclusion. First, competition in mature categories may lead firms to advertise above the level that is optimum given consumer response for advertising of mature brands. That is, the fear of being overwhelmed by competitors' ads may lead them to advertise, even when they observe declining or negative returns to that advertising. Second, new products or brands represent a new stimulus to consumers. As such, consumers' native curiosity or desire for variety may lead them to pay more attention to such ads. Third, new products often represent an entirely new category. As such, competition may be less for such brands leading to less noise in the category. Chapter 7 summarizes the studies that support this premise.

A good example is Altoids. Altoids was a very old UK brand of strongly flavored mints, little known in the United States. To launch the brand in the United States, the firm adopted a campaign with the tagline "The Curiously Strong Mint." The campaign consisted of a series of attention-grabbing, single-page print ads, which highlighted its unique attribute, the strong flavor. The campaign was so successful that it not only entrenched the brand in the United States but also created a whole new category of strongly flavored mints.

Advertising affects loyals and nonusers differently.

Loyals are consumers who repeatedly buy one brand, and *nonusers* are those who have not ever tried or do not now use the brand. Loyals respond to advertising for their preferred brand more quickly and immediately at low levels of advertising than do nonusers. The reason is that loyals are more likely to pay attention to, understand, agree with, and respond positively to messages of advertising for the brand to which they are loyal. However, by that same measure, they are also likely to be saturated with repetitive advertising for the brand sooner than would nonusers of the brand. Thus, they need relatively low levels of advertising for a brand to which they are loyal compared to nonusers of the brand. On the other hand, while nonusers may not respond much to low levels of advertising for a brand they do not use, heavy repetition of such advertising is more likely to gain their attention and affect them more positively than it would the loyal users of the same brand. Chapter 8 explains this issue in greater detail.

Notes

1.   For example, see Kilbourne, Jean (1999), *Deadly Persuasion: Why Women and Girls Must Fight the Addictive Power of Advertising*, New York: Free Press.

2.   Krugman, Herbert E. (1972), "Why Three Exposures May Be Enough," *Journal of Advertising Research* (February), 21-25.

3.   Jones, John Philip (1995), "Single-Source Research Begins to Fulfill Its Promise," *Journal of Advertising Research* (May/June), 9-16.

4.   Packard, Vance (1957), *Hidden Persuaders*, New York: Pocket Books.

5.   See http://www.lawpublish.com/fcc1.html.

6.   McQuarrie, Edward F., and David Glen Mick (1992), "On Resonance: A Critical Pluralistic Inquiry Into Advertising Rhetoric," *Journal of Consumer Research*, 19 (September), 180-197.

7.   Kilbourne, Jean (1995), *Slim Hopes: Advertising and the Obsession With Thinness*, Northampton, MA: Media Education Foundation.

8.   Kover, Arthur J. (1995), "Copywriters' Implicit Theories of Communication: An Exploration," *Journal of Consumer Research*, 21, 4 (March), 596-611.

9.   Garfield, Bob (2003), *And Now a Few Words From Me*, New York: McGraw-Hill.

10.   For a detailed discussion of this thesis, see Aaker, David A., and James M. Carman (1982), "Are You Over Advertising?" *Journal of Advertising Research*, 22, 4 (August-September), 57-70.

11.   Sethuraman, Raj, and Gerard J. Tellis (1991), "An Analysis of the Tradeoff Between Advertising and Pricing," *Journal of Marketing Research*, 31, 2 (May), 160-174.

12.   See Chapter 6 for details.

13.   Tellis, Gerard J. (2002), "Absolute Success" (case for classroom discussion), Marshall School of Business, University of Southern California.

14.   See Chapter 6 for details.

15.   The term *aggregate* means advertising data that have been summed over a large time period (year or quarter) even though advertising occurs over small time periods (e.g., days or hours).

16.   The term *disaggregate* means advertising data that are at the level of very small time periods at which they occur (e.g., days or hours).

17.   See Chapter 6 for details.

18.   See Chapter 7 for details.

19.   Tellis, Gerard J. (1998), *Advertising and Sales Promotion Strategy*, Reading, MA: Addison-Wesley; Colvin, Geoffrey (1984), "Long Hours Plus Bad Pay = Great Ads," *Fortune*, July 23, 110, 77.

20.   Tellis, *Advertising and Sales Promotion Strategy*.

21.   See Chapter 8 for details.

22.   Goldenberg, Jacob, David Mazursky, and Sorin Solomon (1999), "Creativity Templates: Towards Identifying the Fundamental Schemes of Quality Advertisements," *Marketing Science*, 8, 3, 331-351.

23.   Supporting details for all these contingent effects are in Chapter 7.

3

A General Theory of Firms' Advertising

This chapter builds a general theory of advertising, which tries to answer three key questions about how advertising works: Why do firms need to advertise? Why are big successes so rare? Why do firms often continue with ineffective ads?

Why Firms Advertise: Theory of Advertising Demand

Firms use advertising to persuade consumers about the merits of their products. They need to do so whenever supply exceeds demand, knowledge about the supplier or product is low, confidence in the supplier or product is low, or demand exceeds supply.

SUPPLY EXCEEDS DEMAND

The phenomenon of excess supply over demand, for goods and services, is a key characteristic of mature markets, in developed economies, during peacetime. In such markets, technology is sufficiently standardized that many suppliers can produce goods of similar quality. As a result, suppliers have excess capacity so that they can easily increase output. Common examples are more cars than buyers of cars, more workers than jobs, or more candidates than seats on an assembly. In these situations, consumers have abundant choices for goods and have difficulty not in obtaining the goods, but in finding the one that best meets their needs at the lowest price. In such situations, suppliers resort to advertising to persuade buyers of the merits of their own brand of the product.

This premise does not mean that the product is of superior quality. It may be of superior or inferior quality compared to competitive offerings. However, if the advertiser tries to communicate superior value when it is not there, the advertising may be deceptive and is likely to become counterproductive. Yet it is still advertising, and firms still resort to it.

KNOWLEDGE ABOUT THE SUPPLIER OR PRODUCT IS LOW

Knowledge about a supplier or product is low because of the small size or relative insignificance of the supplier, the large number of sellers, or the limited time a buyer has to search for sellers. This could occur even during scarcity. For example, many professionals long for simple software that enables them to easily synchronize their home and office computers. FastMove from Smith Micro Software, Inc., is one such product, which is little known. Thus, FastMove has high potential demand but suffers from low awareness. Advertising can bridge this gap to increase sales and satisfy consumers' real needs.

CONFIDENCE IN THE SUPPLIER OR PRODUCT IS LOW

A situation similar to that described above occurs in the case of a good product from a new supplier. Consumers typically do not know enough about a new supplier to have confidence in buying its product. In this case, advertising could provide information to reduce the consumers' uncertainty or it could provide other signals (e.g., endorsements) to build consumers' trust. For instance, Neutrogena advertises its product as dermatologist recommended for acne-prone skin. In the skin-care category that is cluttered with many brands each spending millions on advertising, Neutrogena was able to earn the credibility of consumers, by relying on this professional endorsement.[1]

DEMAND EXCEEDS SUPPLY

In some situations, demand may greatly exceed supply. Such situations occur when for moral, regulatory, or other reasons firms cannot raise the price of the product so that demand and price are in equilibrium. Examples of such a situation are water shortages during a drought or gas shortages during an emergency. Advertising can serve to reduce demand, for example, by encouraging consumers to conserve water. In this case, the firm may resort to advertising to maintain consumers' long-term satisfaction and not have to ration the product to consumers. Alternatively, a government body may advertise to reduce demand. It could thus avoid the cost of rationing or the growth of a black market. For instance, the California state government spent $20 million on a statewide ad campaign urging Californians to save energy and to shift energy-intensive activities, such as washing clothes and vacuuming, to after 7 p.m. Large retail stores responded to this campaign by cutting their electricity usage.[2]

Why Big Successes Are Rare: Theory of Advertising Effectiveness

Advertisers and their agencies strive to develop creative advertising. They do so while investing enormous resources in terms of hiring, retaining, and supporting scarce talent, researching markets, and testing ads. Every advertiser works to develop a winning campaign. Every creative artist dreams of designing the award-winning, revolutionary ad. Given this enormous effort, we assume that published ads are reasonably well designed. (How to design good ads is a major issue, which is partly covered in Chapters 8 to 11 of this book.) Yet only a few ads rise above the level of noise to grab attention. Only a few ad campaigns become big successes. Many ads or ad campaigns are just modestly effective. Much advertising as practiced today is ineffective. (Chapter 6 provides support for these conclusions.)

Why does this happen? There are probably four main reasons: inattention to advertising, resistance to persuasion, miscomprehension of ad messages, and imitation of effective techniques.

INATTENTION TO ADVERTISING

Consumers can be classified into four distinct states of attentiveness to ads: search, active processing, passive processing, and avoidance. Most consumers are in a state of avoidance. Thus, consumers' lack of interest and active avoidance of advertising are the major reasons why advertising tends not to be effective. To better appreciate this problem, I first describe the various states of consumers' receptivity to ads.

Search

The term *search* refers to consumers' explicit efforts to collect information about various brands of a product, which they plan to purchase. An example is a consumer intending to buy a midsized car who surfs the net looking for information about the best brand in the category. Generally, consumers are more likely to search for information for goods that are expensive, infrequently purchased, or complex, such as automobiles, appliances, or vacations. For example, one survey found that consumers' checking of ads for information increased from 14% for the purchases of low-priced products ($5 to $9) to 46% for the purchases of high-priced products (more than $50).[3]

Drawing the attention of consumers searching for information is not a major problem for advertisers. The key challenges are to provide these consumers with credible information and to persuade them that their brand is superior to the competition's.

However, contrary to popular perception, many consumers do not resort to active search even for expensive and infrequently purchased products. For example, search went up to only 46% for high-priced products in the above study. That figure means that a majority of consumers do not shop even for high-priced products. The main reasons for this lack of search are consumers' loyalty or inertia for brands they use, the high cost of search, or the lack of interest in search. Note that the flip side of the results of the study just cited is that consumers do not check ads 54% to 86% of the time depending on the cost of the item.

Active Processing

Active processing is a state in which consumers think about messages they receive, although they do not make an effort to get this information on their own. An example is a reader of a story in *Time* magazine who reads the detailed copy in an ad for a Viewsonic monitor because he thinks he might like to buy one later. Here again, the advertiser is in an advantageous position because consumers would follow ads for these products on their own motivation. The major concern for advertisers is the proper placement of the ads and the provision of persuasive information.[4]

Until about the mid-1960s, the dominant assumption of advertising researchers was that most consumers were active processors, so that advertising achieved its goal of persuasion through information and argument. More recently, advertisers have come to realize that consumers may at best be passive processors of their ads.

Passive Processing

Passive processing is a state in which consumers receive messages but do not actively process these messages. They also neither seek out nor avoid such messages. Passive processing is also called low-involvement processing. The vast majority of ads for low-cost, frequently purchased products, such as beer, soap, cereals, and tissues, typically win this level of receptivity from consumers.

Consumers may engage in passive processing for several reasons. They may not see the benefit of searching for information about low-priced products, they may feel they already have enough information about such frequently purchased products, or they may just be disinclined to follow such ads. The challenge to advertisers is to gain and retain the attention of consumers who are in this state.

Avoidance

Avoidance is the state in which consumers consciously avoid ads. Consumers may avoid an ad for several reasons. First, it may be for low-priced, frequently purchased products about which they want no more information. Second, they may be so engrossed in the program in which the ad appears that they find the ad a distraction. Third, they may be so loyal to a rival brand that they do not want opposing information. Fourth, they may find the ad boring, stale, or offensive.

Advertisers have always had a problem dealing with consumers who try to avoid ads. For a long time, the broadcast media (radio and TV) had an advantage over the print media (magazines and newspapers) in that consumers could not avoid the ads easily. They could do so only by attending to some other activity or leaving the room. For example, studies estimate that 20% to 33% of a TV audience leaves the room during commercial breaks.[5] One study estimates that even when present in the room, only 31% of viewers pay full attention to the TV.[6]

Now, new technologies have empowered consumers with tools to easily avoid ads even in the broadcast media. For example, zipping and zapping have been in vogue for many years and are probably highest during the interval between programs.[7] Recently, TIVo and Replay TV allow consumers to see programs at the time of their choosing without the commercials. Satellite and cable TV provide consumers with a rich set of alternatives stations from which to choose to minimize their exposure to ads.

Conclusion

Although most consumers consider advertising essential for businesses, they typically are not yearning for ads.[8] A few consumers search the media for ads. Ads humor some and bore others. Many consumers dislike ads, and most try to avoid them. As such, most consumers are in a state of low receptivity for the products of any one seller. This low receptivity is a prime reason for ineffective ads and represents the greatest challenge for advertisers.

RESISTANCE TO PERSUASION

Many people think that advertising is a strong force that firms use surreptitiously or subliminally to persuade consumers to buy their products.[9] Some critics believe that advertisers hold a spell over consumers that they must learn to overcome.[10] However, the truth, as many advertisers will quickly admit, is that persuasion is very tough. It is difficult to change consumer perceptions. It is even more difficult to persuade consumers to adopt a new opinion, attitude, or behavior. Why does this happen? The reason is the selectivity of consumer attention, perception, interpretation, and retention.

Selective Attention

Most consumers are bombarded by a large number of messages or stimuli that clamor for their attention each day. The messages include information from books and magazines; communications from friends, relatives, or business associates; interactions with store clerks or bus drivers; and commercials on the various media such as TV, newspapers, or billboards. Some studies estimate that consumers are exposed to hundreds of commercials and messages each day.[11] Several of these messages require simultaneous attention. So how do people cope with all these messages?

The principle of selective attention holds that consumers simply ignore most messages and focus on only a few, usually one at a time. Why does this happen? There are at least three explanations for consumers' selective attention: pragmatism, consumer liking, and cognitive consistency.

At the most basic level, we can explain selective attention by pragmatism. Consumers cannot focus on two or more things at the same time, much less pay attention to the numerous messages clamoring for attention every day. Efficiency and even survival requires that they attend selectively to the most relevant stimuli. Thus, they tend to screen out all save the few ads most relevant to a purchase they are going to make or have just made.

A second explanation for selective attention is preference. Consumers are more likely to pay attention to subjects that they like, are familiar with, or have experienced. For example, a sports enthusiast is likely to pick an issue of *Sports Illustrated* and see ads for sporting goods or sporting events. An investor is likely to pick up the *Wall Street Journal* and notice ads for new stock issues.

A third explanation is that individuals are selective in attention to maintain cognitive consistency or harmony between their knowledge and behavior.[12] For example, consider a consumer who has just bought a Honda Accord. Such a consumer is more likely to be receptive to ads for the Honda Accord than to those for the rival Toyota Camry.

Selective Perception

Perception is a process by which an individual becomes aware of external objects or stimuli. Individuals realize that these objects lie in a world external to the mind. Based on that fact, they often think that the meaning of those objects lies in the objects, or in the external stimuli themselves. However, meaning lies in the mind of consumers. When faced with some external stimulus that impinges on a sense, consumers compare the perception of that stimulus to similar images that reside in memory. If there is a match, the stimulus gets the meaning retained in the mind for such stimuli.

Thus, prior images in the mind exert a great influence on what meaning a consumer derives from a stimulus. Due to this process, consumer perception of new stimuli gets very selective. Consumers tend to derive those meanings from stimuli that are compatible with the ones in their mind. An advertiser, trying to convince consumers to change their perceptions, faces a big hurdle of consumers selectively perceiving meanings that are compatible with their prior perceptions of the brand or the world. Similarly, research has found that during elections in the United States, incumbents win 90% of the time.[13] Thus, voters' familiarity with the incumbent seems to overcome any appeal or advertising by new candidates.

Selective Interpretation

Often, the external stimuli are complex, and drawing meaning from them requires a certain degree of interpretation. In such a situation, consumers rely even more strongly on their prior beliefs and behavior to make sense of ambiguous external stimuli. When an advertiser presents evidence to persuade consumers of a new position, consumers may reinterpret that evidence to be consistent with their prior beliefs and behavior rather than those of the advertiser. In this way, the advertiser's persuasive appeals can easily lead to minimal change in the audience.

For example, consider the different reactions of smokers and nonsmokers exposed to ads showing that smoking causes cancer. Nonsmokers tend to reassure themselves that they have made the right choice in not ever smoking or in having given up smoking. However, some hard-core smokers dismiss the ads as spouting mere statistics that do not support causality. Other smokers might even go so far as to cite the ad as part of a conspiracy to deprive them of their rights. In this case, the prior behavior of subjects leads to different interpretations of the same message.

Selective Retention

Action in response to advertising depends on consumers remembering a message relayed in advertising. Here again, selectivity exerts a bias against change recommended by an ad. Consumers tend to remember messages that reinforce their prior beliefs and behavior, rather than new ones that an advertiser might attempt to instill in their memory. Thus, even if the advertiser overcomes the formidable barriers of selective perception and selective interpretation, it might still fail to persuade consumers because of the selective retention of consumers.

Thus, selectivity of attention, perception, interpretation, and retention make any form of persuasion difficult. They present advertisers with a huge challenge, especially for firms that want to increase market share or small firms that want to grow.

MISCOMPREHENSION OF AD MESSAGES

A common assumption among advertisers is that most viewers follow the contents of an ad fairly well once the advertiser gains their attention. Attention and persuasion are considered the major hindrances to successful advertising. Proper comprehension of the message is not supposed to be a problem.

However, miscomprehension of messages is another major hindrance to effective advertising. Indeed, a major part of the reason for such miscomprehension may be the selectivity of attention, perception, interpretation, and retention discussed earlier. One study documented the extent of miscomprehension in TV and print messages.

Miscomprehension of TV Messages

An innovative study by two marketing professors, Jacob Jacoby and Wayne Hoyer, evaluated the level of comprehension for regular TV and print commercial and regular programming. The professors tested accurate comprehension of 60 different TV communications (including 25 advertisements) each with a six-item true-false quiz. Their sample consisted of 2,700 respondents aged 13 and over and was reasonably representative of the U.S. population. Their major findings were as follows:[14]

- About 30% of the content of each communication was misunderstood by the viewers.
- The vast majority (97%) of the respondents misunderstood at least some portion of the two communications they saw.
- Every one of the 60 communications was misunderstood by at least some viewers at some time.
- Miscomprehension ranged from 23% to 36%.
- Miscomprehension related only slightly to demographic variables.

Miscomprehension of Print Messages

The same authors replicated their study with print communications. In this case, they used 108 communications, consisting of 54 ads and 54 editorial excerpts. They sampled 1,347 readers who were broadly representative of the U.S. population, each of whom read two ads and two editorials. The testing format was similar to the previous one with one change being the inclusion of a "don't know" alternative. The main findings from this second study were as follows:[15]

- A single reading resulted in 63% correct answers on the questions based on the content of the communications.
- The correct rates are a little higher for ad content (65%) than for editorials (61%).
- At least 21% of the meanings of the communications were misunderstood. This figure is in addition to a 16% "don't know" response.
- With the exception of education and income, most other sociodemographic variables were not related to the miscomprehension rates.
- Regular readers misunderstood the communications just as much as regular nonreaders.

Implications

Many authors questioned the extent of miscomprehension. Some suggested that the single exposure allowed the respondents may have been less than the multiple exposures ads normally receive in real settings. On the other hand, respondents had as much time as they wanted, while ads in real settings may have limited time. Also, real ads are often received with much distraction. Others suggested that guessing on the part of respondents may have led to an increase in estimated miscomprehension by 10%. Even then, the net level of miscomprehension is fairly high. These findings show that besides attention and persuasion, simple and clear communication of a message to an audience can be a major problem. Note that these findings relate to both regular and commercial programming, and to print and broadcast media. Chapter 9 explains how to design copy to overcome such miscomprehension.

IMITATION OF EFFECTIVE TECHNIQUES

Advertising involves a paradox. On the one hand, it largely and routinely appears to be ineffective. On the other hand, it can be hugely successful. Why does it happen? The answer lies in the rare technological breakthroughs in advertising communication coupled with the rapid imitations by competitors of successful breakthroughs.

Breakthroughs in Effective Techniques

To rise above the level of rival advertising, firms sometimes adopt new methods, media, tools, strategies, appeals, and executions. On occasion, some of these turn out to be very successful. This success may be due to the investments in marketing research, the clever strategy of the ad, the creativity of the designers, or sometimes, a small measure of luck.

Alternatively, at random intervals, social scientists may discover new techniques of persuasion. Sometimes, these findings may disseminate through various channels of communication and come to the awareness of advertisers after many years. At other times, advertisers or agencies may learn of these findings quickly through their subscription to research journals or their participation in research conferences. When firms use such techniques to develop new ads, they may produce ads that break through the noise of competitive advertising and are quite successful. This book refers to such successes as breakthroughs in the technique or technology of advertising.

Competitive Imitation

Such breakthroughs, due to the efforts of either advertising practitioners or social scientists, constitute changes in the technology of advertising communication. As in any other sphere of competition, firms are in a constant struggle to come up with such breakthroughs. However, unlike other spheres of competition, breakthroughs in the technology of advertising cannot be easily protected by patent or copyright. On the contrary, they can be easily observed and easily imitated. Knowledge of the breakthrough quickly dissipates through the population of advertisers and advertising agencies. Rivals speed to imitate the successful formula. The new technology gets adopted widely. Imitation decreases the uniqueness of the technological breakthrough and increases the level of noise. The freshness of this new technique of advertising wears off, and its effectiveness dissipates.

For example, when banner ads first appeared in the Internet, their response rate was 10%. Because of heavy usage, by 2002 their response rate had dropped to below 1%. Thus, breakthroughs in the technology of advertising last only for a short period of time due to rapid imitation.

Why Firms Persist With Ineffective Ads: Theory of Advertising Supply

The major findings of the effect of advertising on sales suggest that advertising is not the indisputable strong force many of the lay public believes it is or that professionals hope it is. Indeed, advertisers do not and probably never will control the mind and behavior of consumers to any great extent. Actually, advertising may be often ineffective. If that conclusion is true, one may well ask why firms resort to advertising or why they continue with ineffective ads. Several factors may be responsible for their behavior, including lack of testing and tracking, conflicts with the ad agency, competitive pressure to advertise, the incentive system, the budgeting system, price support, and trade support.

LACK OF FIELD TESTS AND TRACKING

Many advertisers do not adequately test ad campaigns in the field prior to launch or track campaigns that are already running. One study found that only a quarter of advertisers or their agencies evaluate ongoing ad campaigns for effectiveness.[16] Lack of testing may occur for several reasons. First, many ads go through several rounds of evaluation between the advertiser and the advertising agency, including sometimes various forms of auditorium pretests, prior to being adopted. Advertisers may think that further field testing and tracking are not necessary. Second, field testing requires money, and advertisers may not be willing to spend the amounts necessary. Also, advertisers see the expenses of field tests as out-of-pocket expenses. The savings from not spending on an ineffective campaign are opportunities that they may not perceive as sources of income. For example, assume an advertiser has planned a $1 million ad campaign. The $25,000 it takes for an ad test may be perceived as an additional expense over the $1 million, rather than as a small cost that may save the whole $1 million from being wasted. Third, many managers assume that ad testing takes much longer and costs much more than it really does.

For example, when Chiat Day created ads that featured athletes sweating it out, the agency wanted to show an understanding and appreciation of the challenge of the athlete. So every ad told a story about some athlete, while Nike's famous swoosh was hidden in a corner. The agency based that campaign on extensive consumer research. Nike sales grew 30% within the first six months the campaign ran in Los Angeles.[17]

CONFLICT OF INTERESTS WITH THE AD AGENCY

Two forces within an agency may work against market testing: the incentive system and the creative talent. First, when running an ad campaign, agencies provide advertisers with a package of services, which includes carrying out preliminary research, developing the creative, buying media time and space for the campaign, and evaluating the campaign. However, traditionally agencies are paid primarily on a fraction of the media budget used for the ad campaign. Thus, agencies are motivated to execute the campaign with purchases of media rather than to evaluate the effectiveness of the campaign.[18]

In addition, the creative talent within agencies thrives on being original. In contrast, the entire process of market testing may lead to too much introspection that may dampen creativity. Creative executions may also be reluctant to subject their ads to market testing, under the belief that testing will not do justice to their creativity or may not capture all the richness of their creativity. Thus, both of these forces—incentives and creativity—work against the market testing of ads.

To combat these conflicts of interests, several advertisers have recently shifted to compensating agencies on the value of their creative work or the results of the advertising rather than merely on a fraction of the media buy.

COMPETITIVE PRESSURE

Some firms advertise not to gain market share but simply out of fear of losing market share to competitors if they do not. They fear that even if their advertising does not increase sales, it prevents competitors' advertising from gaining market share on them. In this sense, advertisers may be caught in a perceived prisoner's dilemma. All the firms in a market advertise to prevent gains by the other, even though advertising may not benefit all.

INCENTIVE SYSTEM

Often, brand managers are evaluated not on the basis of profits generated but on the basis of sales generated. In such an environment, brand managers strive to win the largest ad budgets they can and to fully spend it as long as they have some hope of increasing sales. They have less of a concern for the effectiveness of their advertising and its profitability. Thus, such firms are likely to have larger advertising expenditures than they really need. Also, they may end up spending on advertising, even though its effectiveness is doubtful.

BUDGETING SYSTEM

Budgeting within a firm typically involves internal competition for resources. Brand managers typically compete for advertising dollars against other brand managers or other competing uses of funds. Managers in charge of various functions or brands must make a claim for resources from senior managers. Such requests are met based on the merits of the proposal relative to other proposals. Despite the overt goal to decide on rational grounds, budgeting does involve emotions and politics. Money is power, and managers need to have that power in order to implement their plans and promote their brands. Thus, they are inclined to make a case for more resources, rather than less resources, for such items as advertising. Such firms may incur advertising expenditures, even though some or all of these expenditures may not be effective.

Moreover, the budgeting system within firms typically moves on an annual calendar. Budgets for a year are set at the end of the previous year. Now, for various reasons, firms may exceed targeted budgets during the course of the year. If a firm does fall short as the year comes to an end, pressure increases on discretionary budgetary items, such as advertising. Thus, managers may be inclined to spend their budgets early in the calendar year, for fear of incurring budget cuts. If that happens, the objective effectiveness of the advertising itself might be of lower concern to the managers.

PRICE SUPPORT

The goal of some advertising may be to support wholesale prices and not to increase sales. The wholesale price is the price manufacturers charge retailers, and the retail price is the price retailers charge consumers. Indeed, some authors argue strongly that, for mature products, the primary benefit of advertising is not an increase in the advertised brand's sales to consumers but an increase in the wholesale price of the brand, even though its retail price decreases.[19] If advertising really has this benefit, then advertising may seem to have no effect on sales, although it has an important effect in increasing a firm's price and thus increasing revenues.

Advertising's effect on price is supposed to work as follows. Advertising increases consumers' awareness and demand for a brand. As a result, retailers are under pressure to stock the brand. Competition among retailers prompts them to promote such brands to consumers with price cuts, in order to bring consumers into the store. As a result, the average retail price of the brand decreases. Over time, highly advertised brands may even become loss leaders, products on whose sales retailers incur a loss. At the same time, because of increased consumer demand for the brand, the manufacturer can increase the wholesale price of the brand. The net result is that advertising increases manufacturers' revenues and profits from the brand but decreases retailers' profits. This effect has sometimes been called the Steiner effect after the author who developed the theory. There is substantial evidence to support the Steiner effect across a number of product categories over several decades.[20]

TRADE SUPPORT

A different goal of advertising from that stated above is trade support. Some advertisers may advertise not to increase sales but to impress their own sales staff and retailers. They hope that their sales staff will feel proud of their product when they see the ads. They further hope that the ads will motivate the sales staff to work harder in order to exploit the potential increase in sales that come from such ads.

Similarly, advertisers expect retailers to better stock the product of advertised brands. In this case, retailers may perceive that the advertised product is likely to experience greater demand from consumers than those that are not advertised. To avoid stock out from a potentially popular product, such retailers may plan on better stocking the advertised product compared to the one that is not advertised.

Summary

In the quest to persuade consumers and win market share, advertising, as currently practiced, is not an indisputable strong force. Indeed, much contemporary advertising may be ineffective. This conclusion does not mean that all advertising is a waste. Advertising is not impotent. Rather, it is a subtle force that firms need to use skillfully to make it effective. When appropriately used, creative advertising can help launch a new product, help a smaller brand compete with a dominant brand, or boost sales of a dying brand. In some favorable circumstances, creative advertising can have dramatic effects.

Firms advertise with the hope that their advertising will have such dramatic effects. In doing so, they draw from the best talent and techniques available in the market. However, when all competitors have equal access to such resources, it is difficult for any one firm to always have an enormous advantage. Even when any one firm breaks out from among competitors with a new approach to advertising, the effectiveness of that approach is quickly diluted by many competitors that copy it. In this sense, the market for creative and impactful advertising is not different in principle from that of introducing new products or picking winning stocks. Many competitors strive to excel with creative and unique ads. However, only a few have dramatic successes, and then too for only a short while.

Given the heavy level of competition and noise in the market, advertisers must strive to make their ads rise above the clutter. To do so, they need to absorb all the knowledge available from scientific studies that show when, why, and how advertising works. They need to test their ads regularly to ensure that their ads are scientifically designed for maximum effectiveness. They need to deploy their limited resources efficiently and effectively, not on the basis of assumptions and beliefs but on the basis of scientific knowledge and tests.

Notes

1. Hoppe, Karen (1993), "Neutrogena: Mass With a Professional Approach" (interview with Allan Kurtzman), *Drug & Cosmetic Industry*, 152, 2 (February), 46.

2. Rivera, Nancy B., and Abigail Goldman (2001), "The California Energy Crisis; Retailers Heed Davis' Call for Conservation; Energy: Stores Hurry to Comply With Governor's Order to Cut Lighting by 50% or Face Fines and Misdemeanor Charges," *Los Angeles Times*, February 3, Home ed.

3. Bucklin, Louis P. (1965), "The Informative Role of Advertising," *Journal of Advertising Research*, 5 (September), 11-15.

4. Rosbergen, Edward, Rik Pieters, and Michel Wedel (1997), "Visual Attention to Advertising: A Segment-Level Analysis," *Journal of Consumer Research*, 24, 3 (December), 305-314.

5. Soley, Lawrence C. (1984), "Factors Affecting Television Attentiveness: A Research Note," *Current Issues & Research in Advertising*, 1, 141-148.

6. Clancey, Maura (1994), "The Television Audience Examined," *Journal of Advertising Research*, 34, 4 (July/August), 38-39.

7. Siddarth, S., and Amitava Chattopadhyay (1998), "To Zap or Not to Zap: A Study of the Determinants of Channel Switching During Commercials," *Marketing Science*, 17, 2, 128-138. *Zipping* is fast forwarding through a replay of a taped ad, and *zapping* is switching channels to turn off an ad.

8. Mittal, Banwari (1994), "Public Assessment of TV Advertising," *Journal of Advertising Research* (January/February), 35-53.

9. For example, see Packard, Vance (1985), *The Hidden Persuaders*, updated edition, New York: Pocket Books.

10. For example, see Kilbourne, Jean (1999), *Deadly Persuasion: Why Women and Girls Must Fight the Addictive Power of Advertising*, New York: Free Press; Kilbourne, Jean (1995), *Slim Hopes: Advertising and the Obsession With Thinness*, Northampton, MA: Media Education Foundation.

11. For example, see http://www.mediascope.org/pubs/ibriefs/bia.htm or Dittrich, L. "About-Face Facts on the MEDIA," http://about-face.org/resources/facts/media.html.

12. Abelson, Robert P., et al. (1968), *Theories of Cognitive Consistency: A Sourcebook*, Chicago: Rand McNally.

13.   Abbe, Owen G., Paul S. Herrnson, David B. Magleby, and Kelly D. Patterson (2000), "Going Negative Does Not Always Mean Getting Ahead in Elections," *Campaigns & Elections*, February, 21, 1, 77.

14.   Jacoby, Jacob, and Wayne D. Hoyer (1982), "Viewer Miscomprehension of Televised Communication: Selected Findings," *Journal of Marketing*, 46 (Fall), 12-26; Jacoby, Jacob, and Wayne D. Hoyer (1990), "The Miscomprehension of Mass-Media Advertising Claims: A Re-analysis of Benchmark Data," *Journal of Advertising Research* (June/July), 9-16.

15.   Jacoby, Jacob, and Wayne D. Hoyer (1989), "The Comprehension/Miscomprehension of Print Communication: Selected Findings," *Journal of Consumer Research*, 15 (March), 434-443.

16.   Lipstein, Benjamin, and James P. Neelankavil (1984), "Television Advertising Copy Research: A Critical Review of the State of the Art," *Journal of Advertising Research*, 24, 2, 19-25.

17.   Colvin, Geoffrey (1984), "Long Hours Plus Bad Pay = Great Ads," *Fortune*, July 23, 110, 77.

18.   Aaker, David A., and James M. Carman (1982), "Are You Over Advertising?" *Journal of Advertising Research*, 22, 4 (August-September), 57-70.

19.   Steiner, Robert L. (1993), "The Inverse Association Between the Margins of Manufacturers and Retailers," *Review of Industrial Organization*, 8, 717-740; Albion, M. (1983), *Advertising's Hidden Effects*, Boston: Auburn House; Albion, M., and Paul W. Farris (1981), "The Effect of Manufacturers' Advertising on Retail Prices," No. 81-105, Cambridge, MA: Marketing Science Institute.

20.   Steiner, "The Inverse Association."

4

Measures of
Advertising's Effectiveness

Advertising can have a variety of effects on human thoughts, attitudes, feelings, and behavior. Researchers have used a variety of measures to assess advertising and its effects. To understand how advertising works, we first need to describe all variables and understand how they relate to each other.

This chapter defines the most common and important measures within a simple classification scheme. It then describes how they relate to each other. Researchers have long suspected that the effects of advertising are related in a sequential chain so that response on one variable leads to response on another. Such a chain of sequential responses is called the *hierarchy of effects*. The hierarchy of effects provides a convenient framework to relate all the measures of advertising. The framework assumes that a relationship does in fact exist between the various effects of advertising. However, researchers have proposed different sequences of variables in the framework. These various sequences constitute different models of the hierarchy of effects.

This chapter first presents a classification of the various measures for advertising. It then presents various hierarchies to relate these variables.

Definition and Classification of Advertising Variables

We can consider the role of advertising in markets as a communication process consisting of three stages: inputs, processes, and outcomes. The inputs trigger certain processes that lead to some outcomes (see Exhibit 4.1). In the context of advertising communication, advertising is the input or stimulus. Its use triggers certain mental processes among consumers, such as thoughts, feelings,

Stage in Communication	Type of Variable	Typical Measures
Firm's advertising input	Intensity	Ad expenditures, share of outlays, exposures, rating, reach, average frequency, gross ratings points, share of voice
	Media	TV, radio, newspapers, magazines, telephone, Internet, billboards, mail, yellow pages
	Ad content: Creative	Argument and other verbal cues; pictures, sound, and other emotional cues; endorsement and other inferential cues
Consumer's mental processes	Cognitive	Thoughts, recognition, recall
	Affective	Warmth, liking, attitude
	Conative	Persuasion, purchase intention
Market outcomes	Brand choice	Trial, repurchase, switch
	Purchase intensity	Incidence, frequency, quantity
	Accounting	(Absolute or share) sales, revenues, profits

Exhibit 4.1   Model and Measures of Advertising Effectiveness

and intent. These processes result in various market outcomes. Advertising inputs and market outcomes are external, overt phenomena that can be relatively easily perceived and measured. In contrast, mental processes are internal effects that are not easily perceived and measured.

This chapter uses the term *variable* in a generic sense to mean a characteristic that describes these inputs, outcomes, or mental processes. The chapter next details the measures for the inputs, outcomes, and processes of the system.

MEASURES OF INPUTS

Advertising is the key input to the system on which this book focuses. It is a force that firms use to persuade consumers to buy their products, in conjunction with other forces, such as price, sales promotion, distribution, or product quality.

Advertising intensity refers to the level of advertising targeted to an audience of consumers. Three important measures of intensity are expenditures, share of outlays, and exposures. Ad expenditure is the dollar total spent by a firm on advertising. Share of outlays is the fraction or percentage of a firm's ad expenditures to that of all the firms in the entire market. Exposure is the number of times an ad is delivered to an individual consumer or household.

Media are the communication channels through which an ad reaches an audience. The major media are television (cable and network), radio, newspapers, magazines, telephone, mail, Internet, outdoor billboards, and yellow pages. Five common measures for the distribution of advertising through the media are reach, rating, frequency, gross ratings points, and share of voice.

Reach is the number of households exposed at least once to an ad in a given time period. By definition, reach excludes overlap in audience due to multiple exposures within a time period. Rating is the percentage of a population viewing an ad in a time period. Gross ratings points (GRPs) are the sum of the ratings from all the ads in a campaign during a particular period. Note that GRPs are not measured but computed as the sum of the ratings of all the ads in a campaign. GRPs are the most common measure for buying media time in market today. Frequency is the number of exposures of an ad in a time period. Advertisers normally deal with average frequency rather than with frequency. Average frequency is the average number of exposures delivered in a period. It is computed by dividing GRPs of a campaign by the average reach of that campaign. Note that average frequency is an abstract term in that very few households would have been exposed to the ads at exactly the intensity of the average frequency.[1] Share of voice is the fraction or percentage of a firm's media distribution divided by that of all the firms in the market. Share of voice can be measured in terms of reach, frequency, or GRPs.

Ad exposure is the most specific or disaggregate level of ad intensity because it measures the delivery of advertising to each individual household or consumer. In comparison, most of the previous measures are more aggregate or cruder. Actually, the order of specificity in these measures ranges from the measure of budget (the most crude) to the measures of media to the measures of contact (the most specific). A valid but infrequently used measure is share of "eyeballs" or share of exposures. The reason is the difficulty that firms have in obtaining these data for the entire market.

The most commonly used measures of advertising intensity are ad expenditures and ad exposures. These two measures are popular primarily because they are the most easily available. For example, firms can easily ascertain the amount of money they spend on advertising from internal records. In addition, with the advent of electronic tracking, firms now often have access to how their advertising budgets translate in exposures that reach specific households or consumers.

Researchers also measure advertising in terms of its creative content. While a vast number of such measures are available, we can broadly classify them into three groups: argument and other verbal cues; pictures, sound, and other emotional cues; and endorsement and other inferential cues. Chapters 8 to 11 discuss the role of these variables in greater detail.

MEASURES OF OUTCOMES

An outcome is the behavioral change in a consumer or a market desired by an advertiser. Examples of outcomes are a consumer's trial of a brand or a brand's sales to consumers. A vast number of measures for behavior exist. They can be conveniently classified into four groups: brand choices, purchase intensity, market outcomes, and firm's accounting variables. Brand choice and purchase intensity are relatively disaggregated variables. Accounting variables are relatively aggregate variables. The order of the variables in Exhibit 4.1 is one of increasing aggregation. It goes from the most specific or disaggregate actions of consumers to the most aggregate at the level of the firm or the market.

The term *brand choice* refers to a consumer's selection of a brand. It is relevant only in a multibrand market. When brand or product purchase can be repeated, we can define three more measures of choice: trial, repurchase, and switch. Trial is a consumer's first choice of the brand. Repurchase is a consumer's purchase of the same brand as occurred on the previous occasion. A switch is the consumer's choice of brand different from the one purchased on the previous occasion.

The measurement of choices in terms of trial, repurchase, and switching gives a complete picture of a brand's appeal. Trial indicates the breadth of consumers' experience with brands in the market, repurchase indicates the depth of consumer loyalty for a brand, and switching indicates a brand's immediate pull relative to a rival brand. One of the major goals of advertising is to create a unique, enduring brand identity. Thus, brand choice is the natural, most relevant variable to measure the effectiveness of advertising. Among the components of brand choice, repurchasing is more relevant to advertising than is trial. The reason is that trial is often stimulated by short-term sales promotions, while repurchasing measures the extent to which preference for the brand endures—precisely the goal of advertising. Nevertheless, any novelty in advertising may trigger brand trial or switching. Novelty may arise from ads describing a new product, highlighting a new or modified product attribute, targeting new segments, or containing new creatives.

When repetitive product or brand purchase can be spread out over time periods, that behavior can be described by various measures of purchase intensity. Purchase intensity refers to the extent a consumer buys a brand over time. It can be measured by incidence, frequency, and quantity. Incidence refers to the time at which consumers buy a brand, frequency to how often they do so, and quantity to how much of it they buy each time. Information on incidence, frequency, and quantity can help to determine what precise effects advertising has on consumer behavior. If advertising changes only the incidence of purchase, then consumers probably buy the product sooner, but not necessarily more often or in larger quantities. As such, their response to the ads is relatively superficial and represents no real gains to the advertiser. On the other hand, if advertising leads to increases in frequency or quantity bought, then the consumer is probably buying more of the product to satisfy higher consumption. This behavior represents a more substantial change in behavior and results in net gains to the advertiser. Thus, decomposing purchases into incidence, frequency, and quantity can provide an insightful analysis of consumer purchase.

The accounting variable is the aggregate of the choices of individual consumers, summed up to the level of the firm. Three important accounting measures are a firm's sales, revenues, and profits. Sales in units are the sum of all quantities of a brand purchased by consumers within a particular time period. Revenues are the product of unit sales and the price per unit. Profits are revenues minus costs.

Relative to the disaggregate measures of brand choice and purchase intensity, the aggregate measures of sales and revenues give a summary measure of advertising performance. They lack the insight into the nature, depth, breadth, or timing of the response to advertising that the disaggregate measures provide. Thus, the disaggregate measures are superior to the aggregate. The aggregate measures are not without merit. First, they are relatively easy to obtain. Often, a firm's own internal records or shipments can provide information on sales or revenues. Second, they may be more accurate, especially if they represent the population and not merely a sample.

Note that price is the key factor that differentiates sales from revenues. Thus, an analyst must take into account the goals of advertising when choosing between these two measures. If the advertising seeks to support or increase price by creating a premium image, then the dependent measure should be revenues. If prices increase sufficiently, then such advertising may effectively increase revenues even if sales decline. But if the goal of advertising is to increase the number of units sold, then sales would be the appropriate measure. In either case, the analyst should observe the effect of advertising on profits. Often, this analysis can be done subsequently, after observing the effect of advertising on sales or revenues, using standard accounting formulas. When doing so, the analyst should hold constant costs that did not change due to the advertising that is being evaluated. In other words, when evaluating the profitability of advertising, only the costs that change due to advertising need to be taken into account.

Market outcomes measure a firm's performance in relationship to other firms in the market. The most common measure in this group is a brand's market share. The market share of a brand is the sales of a brand divided by the sales of all competitors in the market. Tracking market share is particularly important when brands are very similar to each other and the overall market is not growing. In that case, any improvement in a brand's performance can only come at the cost of another brand. This situation occurs in a mature market.

Of all these outcome variables, the most commonly used are sales and market share, two measures of the accounting variable shown in Exhibit 4.1. The reasons for their popularity are that they are easily available and interpretable. A measure that is becoming increasingly popular with the advent of electronic data is brand choice.

MEASURES OF PROCESSES

Processes are mental responses, if any, that occur on a consumer's exposure to an ad. Examples of such processes are awareness, persuasion, and purchase intention. We can classify processes as cognitive, affective, or conative. Cognitive refers to thought processes and includes variables such as attention or awareness. The most commonly used measures for attention and awareness are recall and recognition. Affective refers to emotions. There is a vast spectrum of emotional variables that range from positive to negative and from personal to impersonal. The most common measures for them are liking, attitude, irritation, warmth, and fear. Attitude refers to a consumer's underlying predisposition to act. Researchers sometimes use the term narrowly as an affective variable, and sometimes broadly to encompass all three dimensions of response, cognitive, affective, and conative. Conative refers to variables that are proximate to behavior, such as persuasion and purchase intention. At times the term conative is also used to include behavior.

A key question that has interested professionals in advertising is not the measurement of the processes per se, but the relationship, if any, that may exist among the processes, and between the processes and outcomes or inputs. In particular, the question has revolved around whether consumers pass through any fixed sequence of stages or effects from the moment of exposure to their final behavior in response to the ad. People who think so have designed various models of the hierarchy of effects that describe their beliefs. A subsequent section discusses these hierarchies of effect.

PARADIGMS OF RESEARCH

The distinction between process and outcome variables represents a major philosophical difference in advertising research. Currently, there are two major traditions or paradigms of research: the behavioral paradigm and the modeling paradigm.

The modeling paradigm uses statistical models to determine how advertising affects consumer behavior or market outcomes (see Chapter 5). Researchers in this paradigm generally use advertising budget or ad exposures as their independent variables. They generally use sales, market share, or brand choice as their dependent variables. Studies in this paradigm analyze the effects of advertising in real market situations. Because of their focus on markets, these studies are highly relevant. However, research designs in real markets tend to get contaminated, because researchers cannot control every possible extraneous variable. Thus, modeling studies are not rigorous in ascertaining whether and to what extent advertising is the real cause of sales, market share, or brand choice.

The behavioral paradigm focuses on how consumers attend to and process advertising appeals. It is so called because its interest is in the behavior of consumers. Researchers in this paradigm generally use various ad appeals or formats of execution as their independent variable (see Chapters 8 to 11). They generally use consumers' mental processes to assess the effects of advertising. Researchers typically study the effect of appeals on mental processes in laboratory experiments or theater tests (for examples see Chapter 5). In general, such experiments offer a more rigorous analysis of causality than do studies in the modeling paradigm. However, because such studies occur in theaters or laboratories, their results lack relevance to real-market situations.

Studying the effects of advertising on the processes is important for two reasons. First, the processes indicate why, how, and where in the sequence of decisions that leads to consumer purchases the advertising is effective or ineffective. Thus, they provide an opportunity for advertisers to adjust the content of their ads. Second, the processes can be measured more easily and quickly during ad production. To the extent the processes are related to outcomes, changes in the measures of processes due to advertising may be used as an early predictor of the impact of advertising on the outcomes. Studying the effects of advertising on outcomes is important primarily for reasons of accountability. Most firms advertise in order to achieve certain sales or market share goals. Thus, focusing on these measures is essential for firms to ascertain if their advertising is working and their goals are being met.

Ideally, the effects of advertising should be assessed on both outcomes and processes. Also, an ideal study would want to ascertain the effects of advertising in real markets as well as be rigorous in ascertaining causality. To do so, a study would have to integrate the best of both the modeling and the behavioral paradigms of research. Such studies would provide a more complete analysis of how advertising works and enable a more complete recommendation for action. However, such studies involve considerable complexity. Right now, we have only a few examples that have achieved such an integration. I review them in the next two chapters.

Models of the Hierarchy of Effects

Are the outcome and process variables related to each other in any sequence, so that one variable leads to another? Do the variables constitute a hierarchy of effects? For decades, researchers have been interested in answers to these questions. One of the models of the hierarchy of effects first proposed was AIDA, which was discussed as early as the 1920s.[2] AIDA is an acronym for the four variables involved in the hierarchy:

$$\text{attention} \rightarrow \text{interest} \rightarrow \text{desire} \rightarrow \text{action}$$

The rationale for this model was that a consumer was likely to pass though these stages when going from ad exposure to ultimate action such as purchase. Also, as the consumer passed through the hierarchy, he or she became more likely to take the desired action. Since then, researchers have proposed a number of hierarchy models for different products, consumers, or situations. In an attempt to put some order in this field of study, one researcher suggested that the various hierarchies could be classified into one of three types described as follows:[3]

Learning hierarchy:	cognitive → affective → conative
Dissonance/attribution hierarchy:	conative → affective → cognitive
Low-involvement hierarchy:	cognitive → conative → affective

Note that this classification uses the broader terms cognitive, affective, and conative, for the variables involved, to simplify the discussion of the various hierarchies.

LEARNING HIERARCHY

The learning hierarchy describes how a consumer buys a product only after learning about it. It applies to decisions that the consumer considers important and undertakes carefully. Examples include the purchase of a house, car, major appliance, insurance, or education. The AIDA model is one type of learning hierarchy.

DISSONANCE/ATTRIBUTION HIERARCHY

Attribution theory suggests that consumers develop reasons for their observed behavior, even though such reasons may not have motivated the behavior. The path of the attribution hierarchy is as follows:

purchase → liking → rationalization → brand repurchase

As an example, consider a teenager who buys Calvin Klein brand jeans primarily to be in sync with her peer group. When asked why she bought the brand, she might give the reason for style or looks but not being in sync with her peer group.

LOW-INVOLVEMENT HIERARCHY

The low-involvement hierarchy applies to products such as toothpaste, yogurt, fast food, or TV programs. An example of the hierarchy is the following:

trial → recognition → recall → liking

In such situations, a product category is so inexpensive that consumers prefer to learn about a brand by trying it rather than by an extensive prepurchase study of the alternatives. Consumers can try a brand either through a sample they receive from the seller or through a one-time (sometimes impulse) purchase. If consumers do not like their trial, they can just toss out the item, or not repurchase the brand. Consumers may not try out every brand in the category to determine the best. Rather, they might just repurchase a brand that they find satisfactory. Their prior purchase leads them to recall the brand name, which helps its repurchase. Repeated purchase of this brand ultimately leads to liking. An example of such purchase would be a new or untried brand of cereal, or a new snack.

RELEVANCE OF THE HIERARCHY OF EFFECTS

For advertisers, the most important task is to find out which hierarchy works for their product and sample and what role advertising plays in that hierarchy. This determination is critical to understanding how advertising works and whether it is effective. For example, if researchers find that advertising does not affect sales, they still need to find out where in the hierarchy of effects the advertising began to fail. Was it ineffective in drawing consumers' attention, achieving recall, stimulating liking, persuading, or somewhere else? Researching the role of advertising in this chain of events will give a richer perspective of how advertising works and what remedial action, if any, the advertiser should take to improve its effectiveness.

Summary

There are numerous measures of advertising and its effects. All these measures can be broadly classified as belonging either to inputs, processes, or outputs of a system in which advertising can play a role. The inputs themselves can be classified into three groups: intensity, media, and content, in order of increasing refinement. Outcomes can be classified as brand choices, purchase intensity, and accounting, depending on the level of analysis. The processes can be classified as cognitive, affective, and conative, corresponding to the three different dimensions of mental activity.

The effects of advertising relate to each other through a hierarchy of effects, which is specific for each brand, product category, and consumer segment. Identifying this hierarchy and advertising's role in it is essential to evaluating how, when, and why advertising works.

Notes

1. Although GRPs are mathematically equal to reach times average frequency, GRPs are not computed from this formula. Rather, average frequency is computed by dividing GRPs by average ratings.

2. Lipstein, Benjamin (1985), "An Historical Retrospective of Copy Research," *Journal of Advertising Research*, 24, 6 (December), 11-14.

3. Ray, Michael (1973), "Marketing Communication and the Hierarchy of Effects," Working Paper, Report No. P-53 C, Cambridge, MA: Marketing Science Institute.

5

Research Designs to Assess Advertising Effectiveness

W e can evaluate advertising effectiveness through a variety of methods, which can be broadly grouped into two traditional approaches: the laboratory experiment and the field approach. Each of these approaches has roots in different disciplines, focuses on different variables, and serves different goals. In general, the laboratory approach falls within the behavioral paradigm (see Chapter 4), and the field approach falls within the modeling paradigm. Neither of these approaches is universally superior; each has its advantages and disadvantages. Ideally, using both approaches together, or developing a hybrid method that combines the strengths of each, is better than using either one alone. Most advertising research today relies on either one or the other approach. Thus, thoroughly understanding both approaches is essential to an understanding of ad effectiveness. This chapter first briefly describes each approach, discusses the strengths and weaknesses, and then shows how new hybrid methods can solve some of the problems of these traditional approaches.

Laboratory Experiment

The laboratory experiment is one of the most powerful methods used today to assess cause and effect in research. It has been used extensively in advertising research, especially to determine the role of advertising in persuasion. Indeed, much of the knowledge gained about persuasion (see Chapter 8) and the different routes of persuasion (see Chapters 9, 10, and 11) are derived from laboratory experiments. Thus, understanding such experiments is essential to appreciating much of the knowledge about advertising effectiveness.

This section describes the basic terms used in experimentation. It then explains how one can evaluate the validity of an experiment.

BASIC TERMS

A *laboratory experiment* is one that occurs in an artificial environment, such as a room, as opposed to a *field setting* such as an actual market. An *experiment* is a research setup that manipulates one or more independent variables to observe their effect on one or more dependent variables.

Exhibit 5.1 describes an example of a simple experiment. Here a researcher wants to find out which appeal (argument or emotion) would persuade which of two segments (price conscious or image conscious.) To do so, the researcher recruits four similar groups, each of 35 subjects. All subjects in each group will see only *one* ad. He tightly controls the whole procedure so that all other variables are very similar across the four conditions. He asks subjects to evaluate the news in a 5-minute news program and embeds a 30-second ad in that program. He then evaluates their response to the ad on ad liking and purchase intent. By comparing subjects' responses on these two measures across the four conditions, he can determine which ad works best for which group.

With the help of this example, we proceed to define some other terms used in an experiment. A *factor* is an independent variable suspected of being a cause of the phenomenon (e.g., segment or appeal in the above experiment). A *criterion* is a dependent variable that measures the phenomenon (e.g., liking or intent in the above experiment). The expected relationship between the dependent and independent variables is called a *hypothesis*. For example, we might expect the emotional appeal to work better in the image-conscious segment and the argument to work better in the price-conscious segment.

The *treatment* is a particular level of the factor (e.g., emotion or argument, image conscious or price conscious). The *manipulation* of a factor is the choice of more than one level of that factor. A combination of levels of two or more factors to which one group of subjects is exposed is called a *condition*. An example is the first cell in Exhibit 5.1, consisting of the emotional appeal shown to the price-conscious segment. The *design* of the experiment is the choice and combination of dependent variables, factors, and conditions (e.g., the matrix in Exhibit 5.1).

Subjects are participants recruited for the experiment. The *disguise* is the excuse offered to subjects to recruit them for the experiment (e.g., evaluating a news program in the above example). The disguise prevents subjects from guessing the hypothesis of the experiment and interfering with it. The disguise is not deceptive if it gets information from the subjects that is not of material interest to the subject (e.g., whether an emotional ad is more effective than an

		Appeal	
		Emotional	Argument

Segment	Price conscious	Subjects: 35
		Measures: liking
		             purchase intent
			Subjects: 35
			Measures: liking
			             purchase intent

	Image conscious	Subjects: 35
		Measures: liking
		             purchase intent
			Subjects: 35
			Measures: liking
			             purchase intent

Exhibit 5.1   Illustration of an Experiment

argument ad), and if the researcher debriefs subjects after the experiment about his or her true intent. However, if the disguise gets information that the subject would rather not divulge (e.g., salary, sexual preferences), it could be deceptive.

Assignment is the placement of subjects in various conditions (e.g., in the four cells in Exhibit 5.1). Since subjects are likely to differ prior to their assignment, the research needs to control for that. The most efficient and appropriate way to do that is to ensure that subjects are equally distributed across conditions especially with regards to the dependent variable. To do so, the researcher needs to assign subjects to the different conditions randomly. The term *randomly* means that each subject has an equal chance of being in any of the conditions. A less efficient way to do so is to measure subjects on relevant variables, prior to the experiment, and statistically control for the effect of those variables at the time of analysis. These variables are called *covariates*. However, doing so has two problems. First, if the researcher gets information on the covariates by questioning subjects, that act could alert them to the hypothesis or sensitize them to the treatment. Second, statistical analysis with covariates complicates the analysis and may not control for complex interaction effects among all the covariates and the factors.

EVALUATING EXPERIMENTS

We can evaluate an experiment by its ability to achieve two goals: how validly it can test the real cause and how realistic or relevant it is. The former criterion is called internal validity, and the latter is called external validity.

Testing Causality

The primary purpose of an experiment is to test if the suspected factor is a real cause of an effect or phenomenon. The researcher can do so by ensuring that the only difference among the conditions is due to the treatments. In other words, the only difference in the assignment of subjects to conditions and what they experience in those conditions is the difference in the levels of the independent variables. A laboratory experiment provides a relatively strong test of causality because the researcher can control differences among the conditions or subjects as explained above. In particular, researchers can ensure that

the treatment (cause) precedes the dependent variable (the effect),

subjects are similar on the effect before the treatment due to random assignment, and/or

subjects are measured before the treatment to control for any differences in the dependent variable prior to the treatment.

The two main errors that can weaken causality are history and maturation. History is an error by which subjects are exposed to some other causal variable during the experiment. Maturation is any unexpected and unmeasured change that occurs within subjects during the course of the experiment, due to the form of the experiment. History and maturation weaken internal validity if their effect varies across conditions. History and maturation occur due to poor control over an experiment or due to unforeseen accidents or developments during the experiment.

Relevance

Relevance refers to the extent to which the setup of the experiment reflects the situation in real markets. Most laboratory experiments are weak on relevance. The reason is that subjects are pulled out of their natural environment and subjected to the independent variables in artificial situations. For example, subjects may be invited to view ads in a theater. Even if the researcher uses a good disguise, subjects' viewing of ads tends to be freer of distractions than it is in their normal lives. In addition, the subjects represent only a small and often selective sample of the general population. The researcher does not know how well that sample relates to the general population.

Thus, experiments are strong on testing causality, but weak on relevance. This tradeoff is not accidental but intrinsic to research approaches. As one controls the experimental conditions to ensure a better test of causality, one makes those conditions less representative of the real world, and vice versa.

Field Approach

In the field approach, a researcher analyzes the relationship between any two or more advertising variables from records of their occurrence in real or natural markets, without manipulating either variable. Typically, researchers using the field approach adopt an outcome measure of advertising as the dependent variable, and a measure of advertising intensity or the medium as an independent variable. The typical approach that researchers use to analyze field data is econometric models.

ECONOMETRIC MODELS

Econometrics is a science that tries to statistically estimate economic relationships. This chapter explains the various types of econometric models used to estimate advertising response. Exhibit 5.2 summarizes the philosophy underlying the econometric approach as applied to advertising response. The approach is a system that involves certain inputs, analysis of the inputs, and outputs of the analysis. There are three major inputs to the system: advertising theory, empirical observations, and statistical theory. The system has three major outputs: coefficient estimates, statistical properties, and predictions and strategy implications.

Advertising theory suggests the types of phenomena to study, the types of relationships or paths among variables, and the expected strength and direction of these paths. For example, a theory of consumer response to a firm's advertising may suggest that consumer response occurs at the brand level, primarily in the form of brand choice upon exposure to one or more ads. This theory then suggests a specific model or algebraic equation to capture the relationship. In this case, advertising exposure is the independent variable and brand choice is the dependent variable of the equation.

The researcher must then collect data to test this relationship. For example, he or she could observe the empirical relationship between ad exposures and consumers' brand choices. These observations must then be processed in a form suitable to test the specified model. To do so correctly, one has to draw on statistical theory. This theory suggests the strengths and limitations of various types of data and the appropriate methods by which they must be analyzed.

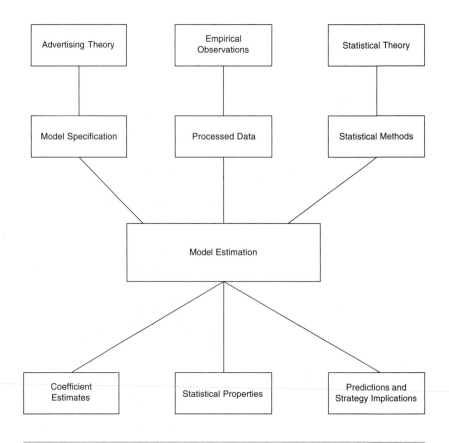

Exhibit 5.2   Econometric Approach to Researching Advertising Relationships

SOURCE: Adapted from Intriligator, Michael D. (1978), *Econometric Models, Techniques, and Applications,* Englewood Cliffs, NJ: Prentice Hall.

Estimation or analysis of the econometric model provides three outputs for the researcher. First, structural estimates of the model's coefficients suggest the precise quantitative values of the relationship proposed by advertising theory. They constitute either a validation or a refutation of the advertising theory. For example, in the case cited above, the estimation could serve as a test of the prior hypothesis about the direction and strength of the relationships between advertising and brand choice.

Second, econometric analysis provides statistics that enable the researcher to evaluate the strength, robustness, and empirical validity of the model. Examples of such statistics are the percentage variation in the dependent variable explained by the model (R^2) or the statistical significance of the coefficient.

Third, econometric analysis can also predict the value of the dependent variable in future time periods. To do so, the researcher would obtain forecasts of the independent variables for those periods. In our example, he or she would need forecasts of planned advertising exposures. By incorporating those forecasts in the estimated model, the researcher can predict what the likely level of brand choice would be for that level of advertising exposure.

One simple econometric model is multiple regression. Multiple regression is a statistical procedure that attempts to determine the effects of independent variables, such as gross ratings points (GRPs) or advertising budget on a dependent variable such as sales. By including into the analysis other variables (e.g., price, sales promotion, seasons, holidays) that could potentially affect sales, multiple regression can statistically control the effects of these other variables on sales, to determine the sole effect of advertising. If the relationship between advertising and sales is still strong, the researcher may then attribute the changes in sales to be caused by advertising. However, the researcher may not assert causality without reservations because of two problems associated with regression: multicollinearity and reverse causality. The next section discusses these problems.

EVALUATION OF THE FIELD APPROACH

We can evaluate the field approach on the same two key criteria that we used for experimental analysis: testing causality and relevance. In contrast to the experimental approach, the field approach is strong on relevance but weak on testing causality.

The field approach is high on relevance for three reasons. First, it consists of real consumers responding to advertising appeals of real firms. Consumers are not recruited as in an experiment. Firms, products, and brands are not contrived as in an experiment. Second, the field approach takes place in a real market with all competing activities that regularly occur in such markets. Thus, what effects are observed in the field approach are likely to carry over to real situations outside the field. Third, advertising exposure takes place in real media without manipulation of consumer attention and processing of these ads. Advertising has to work through all the noise that normally occurs in such situations. Thus, field approaches are highly representative of the real conditions in which consumers see ads and make choices. They are therefore high on external validity.

At the same time, the method is low on internal validity, for two reasons: multicollinearity and reverse causality. Multicollinearity is a statistical condition that occurs when two or more independent variables are correlated. Because of this correlation, the analyst cannot determine precisely which one (if any) influences the dependent variable. The correlation between the independent variables becomes a severe problem if it is stronger than the correlation of either independent variable with the dependent variable. In actual markets, multicollinearity occurs when sales promotions occur at the same time as an ad campaign. Indeed, it benefits a firm to so synchronize advertising and promotion because of positive interaction effects among the variables and increased support from retailers.

Reverse causality occurs when a dependent variable itself also affects the independent variable. The most common example of reverse causality in advertising research is the impact of sales on advertising. Often, managers use a percentage-of-sales approach to advertising. By this method, they set advertising budgets as a percentage of sales. Now most sales are seasonal. As a result, they both are high during seasonal peaks, and they both are low during seasonal lows. A positive correlation between advertising and sales could mean that advertising causes sales or that managers set advertising in expectations of sales. In the latter case, the expected sales pattern causes the advertising level. This relationship is called reverse causality, because the relationship is opposite to what a naïve researcher would assume.

While statisticians have developed methods to mitigate the problems of multicollinearity and reverse causality, these solutions involve various assumptions or introduce other errors into the analysis. In fact, if an analyst tries to determine causality from existing data, the results cannot be valid if the data themselves are deficient. No statistical analysis can fully remedy a data problem. In the final analysis, good data alone can reveal the true effects of advertising. If these data are seriously deficient, then the best solution is to collect fresh data.

Hybrid Approaches

The preceding discussion suggests that laboratory experiments and field research involve an essential tradeoff on internal and external validity. Laboratory experiments are strong on internal validity but weak on external validity. In contrast, field research is strong on external validity but weak on internal validity. Can we combine the two approaches so as to capture the strengths of each and mitigate their weaknesses? Is there a hybrid approach that lies between the two that has at least some superior characteristics?

The answer is yes. There are a few approaches that can serve this task. Two of these are the market experiment and single-source data.

MARKET EXPERIMENTS

A market experiment, also called a field experiment, is an experiment run in the field. In this approach, a researcher manipulates a few independent variables across time or across markets, to observe their effects on one or more dependent variables. The essential difference is that the research context is a real market. Thus, the vast majority of variables that affect the dependent variable are not manipulated or changed.

How then does a market experiment test causality? It does so by varying treatments across conditions represented by markets or time periods. These markets or time periods are selected so that all the other variables that could affect the dependent variable remain approximately the same, or can be measured as covariates. The independent variable could be any of the input measures of advertising or other marketing variables if they are suspected of interacting with advertising. The covariates could be marketing variables, especially those of competing brands, such as price or sales promotion. Advertising of competing brands is also a major covariate, which the analyst needs to control or monitor.

Note how the market experiment combines the strengths of the laboratory experiment and the field approach. Because the independent variables and other covariates are manipulated, controlled, or recorded, differences in the dependent variables are most likely due to the treatment. At the same time, because the experiment occurs in the field setting with minimal intervention by the analysts, the test is highly realistic. Experiment is relevant because sales result from the choices of subjects in natural markets. In addition, the measures of the dependent variable can often be compared with values obtained in previous years. If levels of the independent variables and the covariates for those years are also known, the experiment can provide multiyear comparison, greatly strengthening the validity of the experiment and increasing the insight into the phenomenon.

SINGLE-SOURCE DATA

Single-source data are a combination of data components supplied by one market research firm, through a single, integrated system of data collection. Information Resources, Inc. (IRI) pioneered the system and together with Nielsen is one of the major suppliers of single-source data in the United States. To appreciate this relatively new form of data, this section describes the data system, highlights its importance, and explains its uses.

Description of Single-Source Data

The data collection proceeds in several distinct stages (see Exhibit 5.3). First, the research firm chooses a sample of cities in which all major retail stores

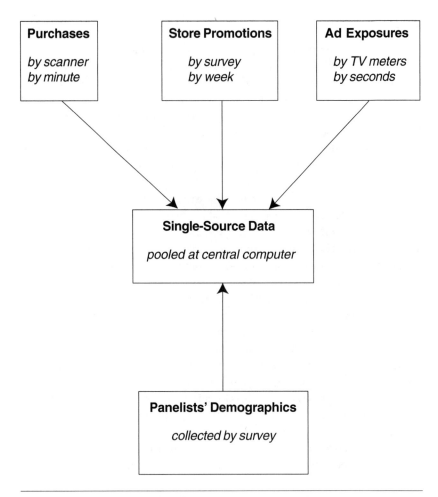

Purchases	Store Promotions	Ad Exposures
by scanner *by minute*	*by survey* *by week*	*by TV meters* *by seconds*

Single-Source Data

pooled at central computer

Panelists' Demographics

collected by survey

Exhibit 5.3   Collection of Single-Source Data

and drugstores agree to provide the firm with access to their laser-scanned sales records to IRI. The firm recruits a sample of households who agree to make all their purchases from one of these stores with a card. This sample is typically in the thousands. The research firm gives all of these consumers a card by which their purchases can be individually recorded as they exit the retail stores. Third, the firm supplies each household with a TV meter that records whether their TV set is on and to which channel it is tuned at 5-second intervals. This tool is the basis for determining TV ad exposures. By combining these records with a separate system that scans for ads in those channels at those time periods, a computer determines the ad exposures of each of the households.

A fourth component of the system, which is not essential for data collection but helps run market experiments, is the IAT. The IAT, or individually addressable tap, is a gadget that enables a central computer to send a cable TV signal directly to a specific household.[1] The IAT enables sample households to receive special test ads through cable TV. The system allows the research firm to run market experiments of TV ad effectiveness, called split-cable tests. In a split-cable test, matched samples of households are sent different levels or executions of an ad campaign, without their knowledge of the research design. Their viewing behavior and purchase behavior can then be tracked to monitor the sales effectiveness of the ads.

When fully in place in any one test city, single-source data consist of the following data components:

Scanner records of panelists' purchases of products, unobtrusively, as they are registered at the checkout counter. These records are highly detailed and disaggregate, containing information on the precise UPC (universal product code) of the brand purchased, together with the quantity, flavor, price, coupons, promotional status, and so on of the brand, and the minute the purchase occurred.

Computer records of the marketing environment in the store. These records cover other brands available, and the price, promotional status, and other marketing variables of those brands. Out-of-store activity, such as retail ads (called features in the trade), are also available in this component.

Demographic records of panelists obtained through surveys. Demographic variables include education, income, family size, and so on.

Ad exposure data obtained through the TV meter. This component of the data includes details of the ad, the time of the day when the ad was aired, and duration of households' exposure to those ads, in 5-second intervals.

Exhibit 5.3 gives an illustration of the data collection via single-source data.

Both Nielsen and IRI provide standardized research packages to clients. These packages consist of selected data, with analytical reports and software for managers to carry out their own analyses. The best-known packages are Infoscan from IRI and MarketScan from Nielsen. The limitations of these data are due to the limitations of the tools used for data collection.

Importance of Single-Source Data

The value of single-source data lies in the fact that it is highly disaggregate across individuals (households) and within time (minute or second). These two characteristics mitigate the two problems of field data, which were cited above: reverse causality and multicollinearity.

Recall that reverse causality occurs because of advertising budgets being set in expectation of sales across various seasonal peaks and valleys. Being highly disaggregate, single-source data contain differences among households' exposure to a brand's ads and their purchases of those brands within these seasonal peaks and valleys. For example, consider quarterly data of a seasonal product such as canned soup. The data may show high sales and advertising in winter, and low sales and advertising in summer. The resulting correlation between sales and advertising is very strong. Yet at the quarterly level the analyst cannot tell if this is because advertising causes sales or whether expectation of sales lead to a certain ad budget.

With single-source data, the analyst has records of individual households' exposure to ads, not only within the quarter but also by the week, day, and minute. Similarly, the analyst has access to those households' purchases by minute. Some of these households do not see the ad at all, while others see it but at different times. Moreover, all households buy at different times. Thus, reverse causality is unlikely to confound data analysis at this disaggregate level of data. By tracking the sequence of purchases that follow ad exposures, and comparing them with those that do not, the analyst can determine whether advertising influences sales. It is extremely difficult for an advertiser to set ad exposures at this highly disaggregate level of households and time. Thus, by comparing variation among households and tracking the time sequences of their activities, the analyst can mitigate the problem of reverse causality.

Recall that multicollinearity occurs when two independent variables are highly correlated. However, due to temporal disaggregation of single-source data, information is available at the minute and second of the event's occurrence. With this detailed level of data, one can more easily discern differences in timing of independent variables thus reducing the problem of multicollinearity. For example, a brand may advertise and have a price cut during a particular week, resulting in a sales increase. Because the price cut and advertising increase occur at the same week, at the weekly level we cannot determine if the advertising or the price cut cause the sales increase. Now consider the same event at the disaggregate level of households. Some households might see the ad while others may not. Within each of these groups, some may receive the coupon while others may not. Each of these four groups may respond differently to the brand. This variation at the household level mitigates the problem of multicollinearity.

As discussed in the previous section, field studies try to determine the effect of advertising on sales after controlling for other causal variables such as price and promotions. In the past, firms used several sources for such data:

their own factory shipments for sales, media-supplied GRPs for advertising, and retailer-supplied prices for price. Such multisourced data were aggregate, sometimes were not quite compatible, and frequently suffered from multi-collinearity and reverse causality. Single-source data represented a revolution in data collection for several reasons.

First, the data are very detailed, giving information by market, store within market, and consumer household within the store. They also provide information by brand, size of brand, and promotional status of the brand. Furthermore, this information can be broken down by week, days within weeks, and even finer time periods if that is required.

Second, the data contain records on all marketing variables that are likely to affect sales such as advertising, price, coupons, in-store displays, and retail ads in local newspapers. Indeed, scanner data contain records on almost 100 variables, versus only about 10 variables in previous data. Controlling for all these potential causes helps determine the effect of advertising on consumer purchases more unambiguously.

Third, the data cover all major competitors in the market. Thus, they give a complete picture of market activity, which was not easily available before.

Fourth, the data are available fairly soon after the records are made. To determine brand sales in the market, the best source formerly was Nielsen's bimonthly audits of retailers. Through single-source data, advertisers can now have access to data within a week after their occurrence, and even quicker if they need to.

Fifth, the data from a split-cable test can be very relevant and provide a strong test of causality. The relevance follows from the setup in which house-holds watch TV ads and make purchases in a natural setting, with minimal intervention from the researcher. The strong test of causality follows from the fact that the researcher can select two similar samples of households in the same market, which differ only by the type of ads administered to them through cable TV.

Uses of Single-Source Data

Single-source data can be used for powerful market experiments in highly natural environments. For example, IRI can split up the sample of households in a city into groups, each of which is shown a different execution of an ad, or is subjected to a different level of advertising. Comparisons of sales across these groups enable the researcher to determine what type of ad or level of advertis-ing provides the best returns in sales in a very natural environment.

Single-source data can also be used for sophisticated field studies and are less susceptible than traditional data to problems of multicollinearity and reverse causality. The reason is that the data can be analyzed at the level of individual households, whose ad exposures are recorded in seconds and whose purchases are recorded by minute of occurrence. Analyses of data at such a disaggregate level are less prone to problems of multicollinearity because different households see ads, make use of coupons, and respond to discounted prices at different times. Therefore, such analyses are less susceptible to reverse causality, because managers are unlikely to target ads to match the precise purchase occasions of individual households. In contrast, when researchers correlate aggregate data, such as monthly sales and advertising at the national level, they could pick up the manager's scheduling of advertising to match sales cycles, rather than the effect of advertising on sales. While single-source data were initially developed for grocery products, their use is rapidly spreading to other categories. Most retail firms now record sales electronically with scanners. It is merely a matter of time before research firms begin to offer systems for single-source data for such retailers and the manufacturers who supply them. Credit card companies, telephone companies, banks, restaurants, and other service organizations also have extensive records of sales by individuals. Some of this information is confidential, and other portions of it are not. These organizations can link the nonconfidential information with records of their promotions to develop their own systems of single-source data. These data can serve to provide new, detailed, and insightful analyses of the response of sales to advertising and promotion.

Summary

Is advertising really effective? To answer this question, one needs to thoroughly understand the alternate approaches for researching ad effectiveness. Two traditional approaches for analyzing the effects of advertising are the experimental approach and the field or econometric approach. Neither of them is universally superior. Because an experiment involves a careful design of variables in an artificial environment, it provides a strong test of causality but is low on relevance to real markets. On the other hand, because the field approach uses real market data, which may not be easily controlled, it is strong on relevance but weak on ascertaining causality. The market, or field, experiment is a hybrid approach that combines the strengths of these two approaches.

A variety of firms supply data or do various types of research on advertising effectiveness. Some of these firms produce tailored studies, while others sell standardized reports on advertising effectiveness. Three important standardized reports are Starch recognition tests, Burke's Day-After-Recall, and

Nielsen's or IRI's single-source data. Single-source data represent the newest and strongest system of data collection because they are observational, highly disaggregate, and provide information on input and outcome variables in a single system.

Note

1. Curry, David J. (1993), *The New Marketing Research Systems: How to Use Strategic Database Information for Better Marketing Decisions*, New York: John Wiley.

Part II

Findings From Market Studies:
When and How Much
Advertising Works

6

Market Effects of Advertising Intensity

A s stated in Chapter 4, researchers have used two paradigms to assess the effects of advertising: the behavioral paradigm and the modeling paradigm. The behavioral paradigm has been used primarily to examine the effects of advertising content on mental processes. This paradigm has been used predominantly in laboratory experiments or theater tests. Because an experiment involves a careful design of variables in an artificial environment, it provides a strong test of causality but is low on relevance to real markets (see Chapter 5 for a discussion). Chapters 8, 9, 10, and 11 review the findings from this research paradigm.

Researchers have used the modeling paradigm primarily to examine the market effects of advertising intensity. Because the focus has been on market effects or outcomes, this research tradition has typically used market data. The method of analysis has been market experiments (also called field experiments) or econometric models. Because econometric models typically use real-market data, which may not be easily controlled, they are strong on relevance but weak on ascertaining causality. Neither the laboratory experiment nor the econometric approach is universally superior by itself. However, the market experiment represents a nice hybrid. If properly designed, it can combine the strengths of the laboratory experiment and the econometric model without being saddled with their limitations. Chapters 6 and 7 review the findings from market studies that have used econometric models or market experiments. In particular, Chapter 6 focuses on the current market effects of advertising intensity. Chapter 7 reviews the findings of dynamic market effects of advertising intensity.

Classification of Studies

Researchers have carried out a vast number and variety of studies on this topic. To meaningfully organize this body of research and summarize the main findings, we need some basis by which to classify them. The focus of various studies provides such a base. Most of these studies focus on one or more of three aspects of advertising intensity (see Exhibit 6.1): weight, elasticity, or frequency.

Weight studies examine the effects of changes in the total advertising across a time frame. *Elasticity studies* examine the effects of changes in advertising from period to period within that time frame. *Frequency studies* examine the effects of changes in ad exposures targeted to consumers from period to period within a time frame.

These three aspects of advertising effectiveness are related. The total advertising budget in a time frame determines how much can be applied from period to period in that time frame. The period budget determines how many exposures are targeted to individual consumers in that period. However, they differ in three important ways. Frequency studies provide the best understanding of how advertising works in persuading consumers to act. Elasticity studies provide less understanding than frequency studies on this dimension, and weight studies provide the least understanding. On the other hand, the implications of weight studies are transparent in terms of actionable guidelines for managers. The implications of elasticity studies are less transparent than those of weight studies. The implications of frequency studies are the least transparent of the three.

Ideally, these three aspects of advertising should be examined simultaneously in one study. However, because response to advertising is complex, researchers have focused on only one or at most two of these aspects at a time. On each of these aspects, we have a stream of research and a small body of findings. To compare studies within a stream and arrive at potential generalizations, this chapter summarizes the findings separately by these three types of studies.

All the studies reviewed here deal only with the current effects of advertising. The term *instantaneous effects* refers to the effect of advertising that occurs in the same time period as the advertising (see Exhibit 1.1A in Chapter 1). This focus contrasts with *dynamic effects*, which consider the effects of advertising in time periods following that of the advertising (see Exhibits 1.1B, C, and D). The next chapter covers dynamic effects. Furthermore, these studies all deal with the effects of the advertising of a brand on the purchases, sales, or market share of the same brand. Researchers have conducted market studies about the effectiveness of advertising since the

Type of Study	Ad Weight	Ad Elasticity	Ad Frequency
Independent variable	Increase or decrease of total ad budget during time frame	Variation of ad budget from period to period within time frame	Variation of ad exposures from period to period within time frame
Target	Total market or segment	Total market or segment	Consumer or household
Response (dependent variable)	Sales or market share	Sales or market share	Sales or choices
Metric of effectiveness	Change in response, if any	Elasticity of response to advertising	Optimum or effective frequency at which response peaks

Exhibit 6.1   Description of Studies on Advertising Intensity

turn of the 20th century, but such research grew rapidly with the popularity of television in the mid-1950s.

Findings About Advertising Weight

The term *weight* means the overall level or budget of advertising in a time frame. Several studies sought to determine whether substantial increases or decreases in advertising weight have any effect on sales and market share. If increases in advertising weight lead to increases in sales and profits that more than compensate for the additional cost of advertising, then the brand needs to stay with that increase. Similarly, if decreases in advertising weight do not lead to decreases in sales and profits that exceed the savings from the lower weight, then the brand needs to stay with the lower weight. Studies that have researched this issue have done so through various market tests.

We need to define some commonly used terms in such market experiments: weight, copy, media, schedule, and audience tests. The word *test* means a specific experiment. A *weight test* is a market experiment in which the researcher compares the effect of advertising between two or more markets, each at a different level of intensity of advertising. Typically, one of these test markets has the level of advertising that the firm currently uses. This market is called the control condition. The other markets are called the test conditions. In the spirit of good experimentation, discussed in Chapter 5, *all other factors are kept as similar as possible between the conditions.*

The dependent variable in these tests typically is sales (or market share). The goal of a weight test is to see whether the increase or decrease in the level of advertising *alone* has any effect at all on sales. In addition to weight, other aspects of advertising whose effectiveness researchers test for are copy, media, audience, and schedule. For example, in a copy test, researchers design ads of different copy to see which one works best. When testing the effect of any other aspect of advertising, the researcher must keep all other factors constant between the test conditions. Researchers can vary two or more variables (e.g., weight and copy) at a time. However, to obtain a valid experiment, the number of conditions rapidly goes up as the product of the levels of the factors. For example, to validly test two levels of weights with three levels of copy, the researcher will need $2 \times 3 = 6$ conditions (see Exhibit 5.1 in Chapter 5 for an illustration of a 2×2 experiment). The term *copy*, in this section, refers broadly to any changes in the content of the ad.

Researchers have carried out more than 450 market experiments to assess the effectiveness of advertising. Six sets of experiments are especially instructive about the effect of advertising on sales. These experiments were associated with Anheuser-Busch, Grey and D'Arcy Advertising, AdTel, Campbell Soup, and Information Resources, Inc. In addition, two advertising researchers (David Aaker and James Carman) reviewed the first three of these studies as well as several smaller experiments. The following sections describe key features of these studies and summarize their main findings.

ANHEUSER-BUSCH EXPERIMENTS, 1963-1968

Two advertising researchers, Russell Ackoff and James Emshoff, described an interesting set of experiments at Anheuser-Busch, Inc., for the Budweiser brand of beer, in the mid-1960s.[1] The experiments varied advertising levels, scheduling patterns, media, and other promotional activity. The most elaborate of these experiments involved changes in advertising weight of −100%, −50%, −25%, 0%, +50%, +100%, and +200% relative to current expenditures. Each level was tried over six areas for greater confidence in the results. The experiments were carried with the support of top management and despite resistance from advertising managers and agents. The latter were also reluctant to accept the results or implement them.

The experiments showed that in the short term decreasing the level of advertising had no negative impact on sales and could actually lead to an increase in sales. The authors attributed the response pattern to the oversaturation of primary segments with past advertising of the brand. They also tried complete suspension of TV advertising. They found that suspension for more than a year led to some deterioration in sales. However, in these situations, the sales levels and sales growth could be restored with just the previous (normal) advertising level. These results suggest the use of a schedule of advertising called *flighting*. Flighting involves staggering normal levels of advertising with periods of complete suspension of all advertising. Cost for advertising can be lower with the suspension, while advertising can be restarted as soon as sales seem to erode.

As regards the effectiveness of different media, they found no significant difference between radio, magazines, and newspapers. However, they found that television was slightly superior to the other media, while billboards were slightly inferior. They also found that promotional expenditures were close to the optimum. Careful implementation of their recommendations between 1962 and 1968, especially about flighting, yielded good results. The recommendations led to a decrease in advertising expenditures from $1.89/barrel to $0.8/barrel with a corresponding sales increase from 7.5 million to 14.5 million barrels.

EXPERIMENTS AT GREY ADVERTISING
AND D'ARCY ADVERTISING

These two agencies reported on a total of 11 experiments.[2] One of these experiments involved reduction in advertising weight to 25% of the original. The reduction did not result in decreased sales. So senior management decided to reduce advertising expenditures over the objections of the brand managers. No reduction in sales occurred in the one year following the cuts in advertising weight. Two tests showed an increase in sales when advertising was increased, but that increase quickly dissipated.

The remaining 8 tests increased advertising in the test condition. Of these tests, only 4 tests showed a sufficient increase in sales that justified a subsequent increase in the advertising budget. The remaining 4 tests showed no increase in sales in response to increases in advertising.

Overall, this set of experiments showed that advertising increases were effective in less than half the experiments and that an advertising decrease had no deleterious effect in sales in the one place it was tested.

ADTEL EXPERIMENTS

Two marketing professors, David Aaker and James Carman, summarized the results of 120 AdTel experiments during the 1960s and 1970s.[3] Panel members had access to cable TV while AdTel controlled advertising by varying either ad levels or ad content to subgroups in each city. Of the 120 tests, 48 were weight tests, 36 were copy tests, and 24 were scheduling tests. AdTel operated a 2,000-person diary panel in each of three test cities.

Six of the 48 weight tests involved lower levels of advertising. Two of the tests ran for more than 2 years, thus having the potential to detect long-term effects. However, none of these 6 tests showed any decline in sales. Of the 42 remaining tests (involving increased advertising), only 30% showed sales changes that were different from the control groups. Interestingly, most of the latter tests were for new products. In contrast, 47% of the copy tests showed significant differences in sales between test and control groups. Most of the weight tests for new products showed significant differences in effectiveness between the test and control groups.

The authors suggested one or more of the following potential causes for the weak effectiveness of advertising:

- Clutter in the advertising environment
- Compensating increases in advertising by competitors
- One third of the advertising tests involved brands with problems in strategy, positioning, packaging, and so on
- Entrenched purchasing habits of consumers

AAKER AND CARMAN'S (1982) REVIEW OF EXPERIMENTS

In the study cited above, Aaker and Carman also reviewed 8 other experiments conducted between the mid-1950s and early 1980s, in addition to the three sets described above.[4] The goal of these authors was to assess whether advertising was effective and whether firms were overadvertising. The authors' analysis included a total of 69 experiments.

Of these 69 experiments, 11 tests involved a reduction in advertising as the key manipulated variable. Almost all (10 of 11) of these experiments indicated that such reductions in advertising had no deleterious effects on sales. Moreover, five of these tests ran for 2 years or more. So they had the potential to determine medium-term carryover effects of advertising reduction. Four of these five tests again showed no negative effect of a reduction in advertising.

Of the remaining 58 experiments, 57% showed no statistically significant effect of an increase in advertising. In addition, some fraction of the remaining tests showed that even though there was an increase in sales due to advertising, it was too small to justify an increase in advertising expenditures. Only a minority of the experiments showed that increases in advertising were sufficiently effective in increasing sales so as to justify an increase in the advertising budget for the tested brand.

Thus, the overwhelming evidence from this review is that many firms were probably overadvertising, at least at the time these tests were done.

CAMPBELL SOUP EXPERIMENTS

Two researchers, Joseph Eastlack and Ambar Rao, reported a series of 19 advertising experiments on the sales of six brands of the Campbell Soup Company in the mid-1970s.[5] Each of the experiments aimed to test the effectiveness of various aspects of advertising. The experiments varied factors such as advertising weight (−50% to +50%), scheduling, media, copy, and target market. Each experiment was a *multiple time series.* Such a design first standardized each market's sales during the test period by sales during a prior calibration period. To standardize for differences due to seasons or other market peculiarities, the authors divided actual test sales of each market by forecasted sales based on the calibration period. The analysis of advertising then involved a comparison of standardized sales of the test market from that of the control market. The various markets were subjected to different advertising configurations during the test period. The measure of sales response was the warehouse withdrawals (of soup) in a particular selling area as provided by Selling Area Marketing Inc. (SAMI).

In the weight tests, the existing target group of consumers received much higher or lower levels of advertising than what they typically received. However, none of the weight tests showed any meaningful increase in sales, indicating that consumers do not respond to mere increases in ad intensity. In two of the experiments, reductions in spending did not adversely affect sales, indicating that budget cuts could be undertaken without negative impacts.

Some experiments involved budget reallocation. Here expenditures were reallocated from highly developed markets to less developed markets. Some of the low-development markets showed an improvement in sales and market share. The result suggests that such reallocation has potential for smaller brands receiving introductory advertising.

Five experiments varied the audience by targeting previously untapped segments. Three of these experiments showed significant positive increases in sales with increased advertising reach. Two of the experiments tested new copy. These experiments succeeded immensely, with sales increases of more than 11% for brands that previously had stagnant sales. The reason for the increase may be that the new copy targeted new users or new uses of the brand.

In summary, the Campbell Soup experiments show that changes in advertising weight had little or no impact on sales. However, changes in copy, media, and target markets did result in sales increases in some situations. Whenever

sales increased significantly, the increase occurred early on rather than after prolonged repetition. The theme emerging from these experiments is that newness, either in media, target segments, or especially copy, is more likely to elicit increases in sales rather than increases or decreases in the levels of the same old ad to the same consumers.

EXPERIMENTS AT INFORMATION RESOURCES, INC.

A marketing professor, Leonard Lodish, and his associates summarized more than 389 advertising tests conducted in the 1980s and 1990s of market experiments at Information Resources, Inc. (IRI).[6] These experiments were part of IRI's BehaviorScan Advertising Tests. In each test market, IRI had established a panel of about 3,000 households, who agreed to make all their grocery purchases by a card and allowed their cable television viewing to be monitored by an electronic device called a *TV meter*. The experimental design consisted of forming groups of matched subsamples of panelists within a market and subjecting them to weight and copy tests.

The authors reported that in 49% of the weight tests, increased advertising yielded significantly higher sales at the 80% level of significance. Now the normal level of significance adopted in most studies in the literature is 95%. The number of test results that would be significant at that more stringent level is likely to be substantially lower, but the authors did not report that number. Even when the advertising was effective at this level of significance, it was found to be profitable (within the medium term of one year) in only 20% of the cases.

An important finding, which echoes that from prior studies, was that massive increases in advertising weight were not more likely to yield better sales responsiveness than moderate increases. The authors interpreted their result to mean that increases in weight alone are not sufficient to make advertising effective. They argued that their results suggest that the sales-advertising response does not increase linearly. However, they did not test the actual shape of the curve. They also found that increases in advertising were more likely to lead to increase in sales when the copy strategy is changed or the brand is in a growth stage.

The authors found that the advertising tests were much more effective for new products than for mature or established products. The effectiveness rate of the tests was 55% for new products versus 33% for mature products (again at the less stringent 80% level of significance). Mature products could enhance ad effectiveness by adopting new copy.

A very important finding from this set of experiments is about the value of repetition. Many advertisers and agencies believe that advertising takes time to have an effect. Another way of stating this belief is that advertising has a long *wearin*. During this time, advertising may not seem to be effective; however,

they believe that repeating the ad drives home the message and ultimately all such advertising will be effective. What the IRI experiments found was that if the advertising was not effective early on, then it would never be effective, even if repeated. Thus, repetition of an ineffective ad does not render it effective. So the wearin period is short.

SUMMARY

The review of experiments is important because of its scope. It covers 450 experiments, by numerous investigators, using a variety of brands, contexts, and time periods. The review indicates that for many mature brands, advertising weight, or the level of TV advertising per se, is not critical in influencing sales. More than half the time, increases in weight alone do not lead to an increase in sales. However, neither do decreases in weight lead to sales decline, at least in the short to medium term. On the other hand, changes in these latter factors (media, copy, product, segments, or scheduling) could influence the effectiveness of advertising. In general, novelty in any of these factors may lead to an increase in sales. Also, ads that contain emotional appeals that induce positive feelings may benefit from increased weight.

Tests that involve a reduction in advertising do not typically lead to a decrease in sales immediately. That could mean that past advertising has some carryover effect that does not decline immediately. Alternatively, it could mean that firms are overadvertising, so that the recent advertising was not effective at all. Prolonged cessation of advertising seems to have deleterious effects in some tests but no negative effects in other tests. Thus, firms should be very careful about sudden, complete cessation of all advertising. If they do so, they need to monitor the effects of such changes closely for a long period of time.

Thus, the overall message from these studies is that advertisers would be overadvertising, at least in targeting the same segments with the same copy, media, schedule, and product. This situation would be exacerbated if advertisers resorted to further increases in advertising weight alone in these conditions.

The experiments indicate that advertising may have carryover effects, though there is less unanimity about the pattern of these effects. Most important, if advertising has any effect, that effect is visible early on. If it has no effect early on, then it is unlikely to have an effect with further repetition. On the other hand, when advertising is effective and maintained over a period of a year, its effects could last at least for two more years. In these cases, the effect in the latter two years could equal that in the first year.

While experiments provide a strong, clear test of causality, they suffer from the limitation of not being carried out in an entirely natural setting or taking into account other competitive activities. The following set of market studies compensates for this weakness in experiments.

Findings About Advertising Elasticity

Advertising elasticity is the percentage change in sales (or market share) for a 1% change in the level of advertising. It can also be called the *elasticity of sales to advertising*. Researchers estimate advertising elasticity by analyzing the differences in sales or market share due to differences in advertising budget from period to period within a time frame.

Like weight tests, studies on advertising elasticity also focus on the advertising budget. However, studies of advertising elasticity go beyond the weight tests in that they determine the shape and strength of the advertising response function. Typically, researchers express this shape as a particular mathematical function and the strength as an elasticity. To do so, researchers use some econometric model of the effect of advertising on sales or market share.

Researchers have conducted a vast number of studies of advertising elasticity. Most of these studies have used naturally occurring market data from research firms or advertisers themselves. However, some of the studies have also generated data through market experiments of the type described above.

Various reviews and meta-analyses have tried to summarize the findings from the original econometric models of advertising response. A literature review briefly describes each original study and summarizes the results across studies. In contrast, a meta-analysis is a study that treats the findings from original studies as dependent observations, which are then pooled together and analyzed by the characteristics of those original studies.

There are at least two major reviews and two major meta-analyses of the effects of advertising on sales. This chapter reviews only the two meta-analyses, for one important reason.[7] The two meta-analyses are comprehensive enough that they encompass the scope and findings of the two reviews. The chapter first provides a brief explanation of the meta-analytic approach and then presents the results of the meta-analyses.

META-ANALYSIS

The formal analysis of the sales effectiveness of advertising with econometric models became popular in the late 1950s. Since then, numerous authors have studied the effects of advertising in a variety of contexts using a variety of research designs. The contexts include different brands, products, stages of the product life cycle, or countries of the world. The research designs include various types of data and models for analyzing them. Despite this variety, fortunately, many of the studies reported their results in one comparable statistic, advertising elasticity. Thus, these studies are comparable.

Given this body of research, a valid question is, what have we learned about advertising effectiveness? Can we summarize all the findings to get some meaningful estimate about the elasticity? Can we tell how this elasticity varies by type of research design or context of the primary study? The answer is yes. The most efficient approach to do so is meta-analysis.

The common mean of advertising elasticity across all the studies gives the best estimate of the effect of advertising in the population, that is, across all contexts and research designs. One formal approach for doing such a summary is *meta-analysis*. In this approach, the findings about the effectiveness of advertising are first expressed in common units. In this case, advertising elasticity is a good measure, because it is free of units and can be conveniently compared across studies. Indeed, by the early 1990s, a variety of primary studies yielded more than 400 estimates of advertising elasticity.

The meta-analytic approach next determines the mean of these elasticities and its systematic variation, if any, due to differences in design or contexts of the primary studies. In effect, the elasticities themselves can be used as dependent variables. The characteristics of the design or context of the primary studies can be used as independent variables that explain the dependent variable. The next two sections review the findings from two major meta-analyses of past advertising studies.

ASSMUS, FARLEY, AND LEHMANN (1984)

Three marketing professors, Gert Assmus, John Farley, and Donald Lehmann, used a form of meta-analysis to identify the variation of advertising elasticity across various contexts and designs.[8] The authors conducted the analysis for 128 econometric models from primary studies that analyzed the impact of advertising on sales or market share. Their major findings were the following:

- Short-term elasticities were much lower in models that incorporated a *carry-over coefficient* (a lagged dependent variable) than in models without one. The reason is that current and past advertising is generally positively correlated and both have a positive impact on current sales; so the omission of past advertising will cause an upward bias for current advertising.
- Models that contained *exogenous variables* had smaller short-term elasticities than those that did not. These variables, such as income or family size, generally have a positive correlation with sales; hence their omission may upwardly bias the effect of advertising.
- Elasticities in *additive models* were higher than those in *multiplicative models*. The reason is that the elasticity varies in linear additive models unlike in multiplicative models, where the elasticity is constant over the range of the demand

function. Now, it is simplistic to expect advertising's effect to be linear. So here again, the use of the wrong model could lead to an upward bias in the estimated elasticity of sales on advertising.

- Pooled data involving cross-sectional observations in addition to time series observations yielded higher elasticities. The reason could be that higher share brands also have higher levels of advertising. Thus, pooling data across brands may lead to an upward bias in the estimated elasticity.
- Food products have an elasticity that is .1 higher than other products. Elasticities were also significantly higher for Europe compared to the United States.
- Elasticities did not differ depending on whether the dependent measure in the original study was sales or market share. Elasticities did not differ depending on whether the original study was for a product or brand. Elasticities also did not differ depending by type of estimation used in the original studies. These lacks of difference are important because they suggest that future studies need to be less concerned about such differences and researchers can more easily pool or compare results of studies that differ on these dimensions.

The grand mean for advertising elasticity was .2. However, this mean does not reflect corrections for factors that could upwardly bias the mean. Unfortunately, the authors did not present a mean corrected for such biases. The grand mean for the carryover elasticity of advertising was .5. The authors acknowledged that this coefficient can be seriously biased by data aggregation in the original studies.[9] However, the authors did not report any estimate of the degree of this bias. Thus, one may not use either of these elasticities indiscriminately.

SETHURAMAN AND TELLIS (1991)

A marketing professor, Raj Sethuraman, and I carried out a more recent meta-analysis of advertising elasticities than the one above.[10] Our study covered 260 primary estimates of the elasticity of sales or market share to advertising. Our major finding is that the average elasticity across all 260 estimates is .11. This estimate is half that of Assmus, Farley, and Lehmann. We attributed the differences to our larger and more recent sample.

What does this number of .1 mean? Strictly, an elasticity of .1 means that a 1% increase in the level of advertising results in only about a .1% increase in sales. Empirically, we also compared this advertising elasticity with the corresponding price elasticity obtained from primary studies that estimated *both* elasticities. The price elasticity is −1.6.[11] Thus, the results of the empirical analysis show that the average price elasticity is about 15 times the average advertising elasticity. Because means can be influenced by outliers, we also compared the advertising and price elasticities based on medians. We found that price elasticity was almost 20 times that of advertising elasticity.

One important finding is the big difference for nondurable and durable goods. For nondurable goods, we found that the median price elasticity is 25 times the median advertising elasticity, whereas for durable goods this ratio is just 5. This result suggests that in the case of nondurable goods, price discounting may probably be a more profitable option than an advertising increase. One reason for this difference may be that consumers are prepared to pay a premium for durable goods of a "perceived quality." On the other hand, for nondurable goods, consumers may be willing to switch to brands that have lower prices.

Based on estimated levels of pass-through and of consumers switching brands for a better deal, we made a rough estimate of the optimality of the advertising in durables and nondurables. We suspected that marketers of nondurables were probably overadvertising, while those of durables were probably underadvertising.

Another important finding is that advertising elasticity is almost half as high in the United States as it is in Europe. The reason may be that advertisers in the United States tend to overadvertise or that those in Europe are not advertising as much as they should. In terms of the ratio of median price elasticity to advertising elasticity, the ratio is three times higher for the United States (19.5 vs. 6.2). This difference may suggest that consumers are much more price sensitive than advertising sensitive in the United States compared to Europe. One reason, again, may be that the level of advertising is too high in the United States. Another reason may be that there is less scope for and correspondingly less sensitivity for price discounting in Europe than in the United States.

We also reported that products in the early stages of their life cycle have a median ratio of price to advertising elasticity of 17.7 whereas those in the later stages have a significantly higher median elasticity ratio of 22.2. This result indicates that price discounts would be more effective in promoting sales in the later stages of the product's life cycle whereas advertising increases would be more effective in promoting sales in the early stages of the product's life cycle.

Findings About Advertising Frequency

Advertising normally works through its effects on individual consumers. Thus, the advertising budget in a time period ultimately translates into a sequence of individual exposures targeted to one or more consumers Similarly, sales may be considered an aggregate of consumers' choices about individual brands. The term *frequency* refers to the number of ad exposures each consumer receives in a particular time period. Effective frequency refers to the optimum frequency that maximizes consumers' purchases of the advertised brand.

Databases that record consumers' choices of brands typically also record the delivery of advertising in the form of advertising exposures. The analysis of consumers' choices presents unique problems and opportunities for understanding the effects of advertising. The major problem is that since each consumer has a large number of purchases, the size and complexity of the database quickly increase with the sample size. However, a focus on choice provides a large number of advantages. The key advantages are greater insight into how advertising works and a freedom from bias that occurs if one aggregates data over consumers or exposures.

Like studies on advertising elasticity, studies on frequency also determine the effectiveness of advertising in terms of the shape of the response function. However, studies on advertising elasticity capture the aggregate response function for the advertising budget. In contrast, studies on frequency capture the response function of consumers' choices in terms of exposure to ads at very specific times. Thus, such studies are far more specific in details and insight. At the same time, they are not immediately practical. Even if a manager knows the effective frequency, he or she still needs to know what advertising budget and scheduling will deliver that frequency to the appropriate consumers. So this stream of research by itself is insufficient to understanding how to use advertising.

Several studies have focused on the effect of ad exposures on consumer choice. One of the first and best known, by McDonald, was on diary data. Most of the others have all been on single-source data. We review the findings from five of these studies.

McDONALD (1971)

An advertising researcher, Colin McDonald, analyzed the diary records of a sample of 266 panelists.[12] Panelists consisted of 255 homemakers, in London, United Kingdom, for 13 weeks at the end of 1966. During that time, panelists kept a diary of the day on which and the medium in which they saw ads and their purchases of various brands in 50 different product categories. The author analyzed the data for nine product categories. He took great care to avoid spurious causality when analyzing the data. In particular, he made sure that he did not interpret the pattern of loyal consumers of a brand being targeted with more ads, as one of response to advertising. To avoid this, he analyzed all his data at the individual panelist level. That is, he first identified within-panelist relationships, and then aggregated the within and then across categories. Three major conclusions from the study are worth noting.

First, McDonald found that panelists were 5% more likely to switch to than from a brand, when, in the interval between two purchases, they had seen two or more ads for the brand.

Second, the above effect was stronger for ads seen less than 4 days before the purchase than for ads seen more than 4 days before the purchase. In other words, the effect of advertising decayed rapidly after 4 days from the time of exposure.

Third, subjecting panelists to three or more purchases did not seem to have a stronger effect than doing so with two exposures. This suggests that saturation occurred at two exposures or that two exposures were optimum. The reader needs to keep in mind that this entire analysis is between purchases of an individual consumer.

McDonald did not compute the advertising elasticity of advertising. However, his conclusion that going from one to two exposures gives a 5% increase in brand choices suggests an elasticity of .05.[13] This is similar to that obtained from the prior econometric studies. McDonald's study is important because of the novelty of the findings, the strength of the design, and its pioneering focus on individual consumers' response to individual exposures.

TELLIS (1988a)

The advent of single-source data in the 1980s allowed researchers to carry out studies similar in spirit to McDonald's. However, with the development of new statistical tools and the far richer detail of single-source data, new studies could far exceed McDonald's in scope and detail. In particular, they could test a number of behavioral theories, which in the past had been tested only in laboratory studies with limited numbers of subjects.

I carried out the first such study in the category of toilet tissue.[14] Despite the almost commodity status of this category, total advertising in the category amounted to hundreds of millions of dollars. I sought to understand how the repetitive exposure of ads affected consumers' purchase of those brands. I decomposed purchase into two components, brand choice and quantity bought. I considered household purchases of 10 key brands of toilet tissue over 52 weeks. The data also included weekly TV meter records of exposure to TV ads, which are determined by the household's TV viewing and a brand's airing of commercials. The sample included 252 panelists and 2,634 purchase occasions.

The first stage is a logit model analyzing the probability of choosing a particular brand, which is actually the probability that the perceived utility of the brand, estimated by certain choice characteristics, exceeds the utility of any other brand. The second stage or the tobit model includes the dependence of units bought on the brand choice. The study had four major findings.

First, the effects of advertising were small and quite difficult to identify. In contrast, the effects of sales promotions were strong, immediate, and hard to miss. The sales promotions consisted of price discounts, coupons, in-store display, and retailers' features.

Second, brand loyalty moderated the effects of ad exposure. Buyers responded more strongly to brands to which they were more loyal.

Third, the response to ad exposure seemed nonlinear. However, brand loyalty strongly moderated this nonlinearity. The response for brands to which the consumer was loyal occurred rapidly and peaked at two to three exposures. However, brands with which the consumer was not familiar required many more exposures per week, but could achieve a higher peak.

Fourth, advertising had a small effect in winning new buyers but a little stronger effect in reinforcing preference. In other words, advertising seems to affect loyal buyers more than nonloyal buyers, causing an increase in volume purchased rather than brand switching. Thus, newer brands need very high levels of exposure before they can induce trial.

This study is important because it demonstrated a method to analyze single-source data rigorously and offer insights for researchers and managers.

PEDRICK AND ZUFRYDEN (1991)

Two marketing professors, James Pedrick and Fred Zufryden, studied the effectiveness of advertising in the yogurt category.[15] They obtained the data from Nielsen's single-source data for Sioux Falls, South Dakota, from 1986 to 1988. Like the study described above, Pedrick and Zufryden also used a multistage econometric model. However, they considered the stages of whether consumers did or did not buy yogurt on a shopping trip (incidence) and which brand was bought (choice).

In a unique and important departure from all other studies covered in this section, Pedrick and Zufryden also included a third model of how consumers were exposed to ads. The advantage of this third model was that it enables managers to determine how to translate an advertising budget to various appropriate levels of reach and frequency. *Reach* is the percentage of the audience exposed at least once to an ad in a time period.

Three of the results that Pedrick and Zufryden obtained are similar to those of Tellis (1988a): The effects of advertising are relatively small, the effects of promotions are much stronger than those of advertising, and the response to ad exposure is nonlinear.

The most important result they obtained is that market share increases were much more responsive to increases in reach than to increases in frequency. From the results provided, a frequency of two exposures per week seemed to be optimal, if the goal was to maximize market share. At levels greater than two exposures, market share continued to go up but at a very slow rate. Much better response could be obtained by using the budget to invest in wider reach than in higher frequency. Unfortunately, the authors did not provide results for frequency levels between 0 and 2.

DEIGHTON, HENDERSON, AND NESLIN (1994)

Three marketing professors, John Deighton, Caroline Henderson, and Scott Neslin, carried out analysis of single-source data using econometric models similar to the two prior studies described in this section.[16] They obtained their data from IRI, for three frequently purchased, mature product categories: ketchup, liquid detergent, and powder detergent. The authors studied the effect of exposure frequency on brand choice of the advertised brand. In the latter model, they focused on the effect of advertising on repeat purchasing and on brand switching.

The authors measured the frequency of a brand's advertising as the number of ad exposures to that consumer since his or her last purchase. Notice that this measure of advertising exposure is the most relevant (of all prior studies), because it accounts for the total advertising between purchase occasions and most affects brand choice. However, this measure is also the least useful for managers, because they do not have an easy means by which to target specific levels of exposures between purchase occasions of consumers.

As in the prior two studies, the authors found that the effects of other promotional variables were much stronger than that of advertising. The effect of advertising was significantly different from 0 for two of the three categories. The authors' most important finding was that probability of a consumer buying a brand increased steadily with the number of exposures, even going up to exposure levels of 20. However, this effect went up at a declining rate. Also, the biggest increase occurred when going from an exposure level of 0 to 1. The authors point out that these results do not immediately indicate the optimum level of exposure. That would depend on the cost of exposure and the margin from the incremental sales generated by response to those exposures.

Thus, one important implication from this study is that higher frequency could be profitable depending on the cost of exposures and the margin structure of the brand. Thus, there is no single, correct level of frequency, a conclusion that the next study seems to assert.

JONES (1995)

Advertising professor John Philip Jones analyzed single-source data for 142 brands in 12 categories in 1991.[17] All 12 were from packaged grocery products and included markets that were competitive and heavily advertised. He focused on the short-term effect of advertising that occurred in the 7 days just prior to purchase. In this sense, the approach is similar to that of McDonald's discussed earlier. Jones first developed a control level or baseline of sales. This baseline consisted of a brand's share of purchases in each category in households that had not received television advertising in the 7 days just prior to purchase. The share was calculated as an average over the whole year, including promoted and nonpromoted categories, and over periods with different seasonalities. As such, effects due to promotions or seasons would be averaged out.

Jones found that advertising does have short-term effects on household purchases of the advertised brands. However, the direction of the effect is not universal. About 50% of the brands have ad effects that are moderate to strong. About 30% have effects that are not clearly distinguishable, while 20% strangely have negative effects. Some fraction of the brands that have a short-term effect also have long-term effects on sales. But long-term effects are much less pronounced than the short-term effects.

The most important result from the Jones study is about advertising repetition. He found that in the 7 days just prior to purchase, the first exposure gets the most response. Additional exposures do not add much. Thus, the conclusion from this study is that "one exposure is enough."

A marketing consultant, Lawrence Gibson, found similar results from analyzing TRI-NET market experiments of 60 commercials at General Mills.[18] He found that just one exposure of an ad was adequate to achieve big changes in attitude and coupon usage for that brand; multiple exposures were not necessary.

This last result, stated as above, has created some controversy and has led some researchers to question Jones's analysis and interpretation. Two issues that are most pertinent are the formation of the baseline sample and the identification of the 7-day period. First, the results of the study are valid only if advertisers do not target households who buy their brands with heavier advertising. If that is the case, then Jones might pick up an effect of advertising, which is merely due to targeting. McDonald took great pains to ensure that his analysis was free from such a spurious correlation. Second, Jones's analysis excluded households that may have received ads earlier than the 7-day period. Thus, any increase in response from those unmeasured exposures remains unaccounted.

In conclusion, Jones obtained some very important results. However, the validity and generalizability of the findings must await replication that is assuredly free of the above two problems.

Summary

This section summarizes the findings from our review of studies on weight, elasticity, and frequency.

FINDINGS ABOUT ADVERTISING WEIGHT

The review of weight studies leads to the following common findings:

- Many advertisers may be overadvertising and should regularly track the effectiveness of their advertising.
- Weight alone is not critical. Increases in weight alone do not necessarily lead to an increase in sales. Decreases in weight alone do not lead to sales decline, at least in the short to medium term.
- Prolonged cessation of advertising shows deleterious effects in some tests but no negative effects in other tests. These results reiterate the importance for determining if firms are overadvertising in the short term.
- If advertising has any effect, that effect is visible early on. If it has no effect early on, then it is unlikely to have an effect with further repetition.
- Changes in media, copy, product, segments, or scheduling are much more likely to lead to changes in sales than do changes in weight.

FINDINGS ABOUT ADVERTISING ELASTICITY

The review of elasticity studies leads to the following major substantive findings:

- The grand mean of advertising elasticity is .1. In comparison, price elasticity is about 15 times higher in magnitude but opposite in direction.
- Advertising elasticity is higher in the early stages of the life cycle than in the latter stages.
- Food products have an elasticity that is .1 higher than other products.
- Elasticities in the United States are almost half those in Europe.
- The ratio of the median price to advertising elasticity for nondurables is five times that for durables.
- These results suggest that marketers of nondurables are probably overadvertising, and those of durable goods are probably underadvertising.

The review of elasticity studies leads to the following major methodological findings:

- Short-term elasticities are much lower in models that incorporated a carryover coefficient (a lagged dependent variable) than in models without one.
- Models that contained exogenous variables had smaller short-term elasticities than those that did not.
- Elasticities in additive models were higher than those in multiplicative models.
- Pooled data involving cross-sectional observations in addition to time series observations yielded higher elasticities.
- Elasticities did not differ by the measure of the dependent variable in the original study, whether sales or market share.

- Elasticities did not differ by the subject of the original study, whether product or brand.
- Elasticities also did not differ by type of estimation in the original studies.

FINDINGS ABOUT ADVERTISING FREQUENCY

The studies on frequency suggest some convergence on the following main findings:

- The effects of ad exposure on choice are much less prominent than those for price and sales promotions.
- Higher frequency of ad exposures leads to increased probability of purchase.
- Purchase probability exhibits a concave response to higher ad frequency. That is, the probability of purchase increases but at a decreasing rate.
- For mature, frequently purchased products, the optimum level of exposure tends to be relatively small, ranging from one to three exposures a week.

Some important but unique findings, not replicated across studies, are the following:

- Brand familiarity or loyalty moderates response to ad exposures. That is, more established brands have a different response to ad exposures than newer brands. In particular, older established brands have an earlier and lower peak response to ad exposures than newer brands.
- Purchase probability may be more responsive to reach than to frequency.

Notes

1. Ackoff, Russell L., and James R Emshoff (1975), "Advertising at Anheuser-Busch, Inc. (1963-68)," *Sloan Management Review,* 16, 2 (Winter), 1-16.
2. As reviewed in Aaker, David A., and James M. Carman (1982), "Are You Over Advertising?" *Journal of Advertising Research,* 22, 4 (August/September), 57-70.
3. Ibid.
4. Ibid.
5. Eastlack, Joseph O., Jr., and Ambar G. Rao (1989), "Advertising Experiments at the Campbell Soup Company," *Marketing Science,* 8 (Winter), 57-71.
6. Abraham, Magid, and Leonard Lodish (1989), *Advertising Works: A Study of Advertising Effectiveness and the Resulting Strategic and Tactical Implications,* Chicago: Information Resources, Inc.; Lodish, Leonard M., et al. (1995), "How T.V. Advertising Works: A Meta-Analysis of 389 Real World Split Cable T.V. Advertising," *Journal of Marketing Research,* 32 (May), 125-139; Lodish, Leonard M., et al. (1995), "A Summary of Fifty-Five In-Market Experimental Estimates of the Long-Term Effect of TV Advertising," *Marketing Science,* 14, 3, Part 2 of 2, G133-G139.
7. The two reviews of econometric studies that are not covered here are Aaker and Carman, "Are You Over Advertising?" and Leone, Robert, and Randall L. Schultz (1980), "A Study of Marketing Generalization," *Journal of Marketing,* 44 (Winter), 10-18.

8.   Assmus, Gert, John U. Farley, and Donald R. Lehmann (1984), "How Advertising Affects Sales: Meta-Analysis of Econometric Results," *Journal of Marketing Research*, 21 (February), 65-74.

9.   A study by Clarke (1976) indicates the level of this bias and how to compute it. See Clarke, Darryl G. (1976), "Econometric Measurement of the Duration of Advertising Effect on Sales," *Journal of Marketing Research*, 13 (November), 345-357.

10.   Sethuraman, Raj, and Gerard J. Tellis (1991), "An Analysis of the Tradeoff Between Advertising and Pricing," *Journal of Marketing Research*, 31, 2 (May), 160-174. See also Tellis, Gerard J. (1988b), "The Price Elasticity of Selective Demand," *Journal of Marketing Research*, 25, (November), 331-341.

11.   See also Tellis, "The Price Elasticity."

12.   McDonald, Colin (1971), "What Is the Short-Term Effect of Advertising?" Marketing Science Institute Report No. 71-142, Cambridge, MA: Marketing Science Institute.

13.   Percentage change in response = 5. Percentage change in advertising = 100. Elasticity = 5/100, or .05.

14.   Tellis, Gerard J. (1988a), "Advertising Exposure, Loyalty and Brand Purchase: A Two Stage Model of Choice," *Journal of Marketing Research*, 15, 2 (May), 134-144.

15.   Pedrick, James H., and Fred S. Zufryden (1991), "Evaluating the Impact of Advertising Media Plans: A Model of Consumer Purchase Dynamics Using Single Source Data," *Marketing Science*, 10, 2 (Spring), 111-130.

16.   Deighton, John, Caroline Henderson, and Scott Neslin (1994), "The Effects of Advertising on Brand Switching and Repeat Purchasing," *Journal of Marketing Research*, 31 (February), 28-43.

17.   Jones, John Philip (1995), "Single-Source Research Begins to Fulfill Its Promise," *Journal of Advertising Research* (May/June), 9-15.

18.   Gibson, Lawrence (1996), "What Can One Exposure Do?" *Journal of Advertising Research*, (March/April), 9-18.

7

Advertising's Dynamic and Content Effects

M arket studies on advertising effectiveness have focused on three other aspects of advertising, in addition to the three discussed in the previous chapter: carryover effects of advertising, wearin and wearout, and the effects of ad content. This chapter uses the term *dynamics* to refer jointly to the issues of carryover, wearin, and wearout, because they deal with the effects of advertising over time. The chapter next reviews studies on each of these three topics.

Findings About Advertising Carryover

The analysis of advertising carryover is important for several reasons. First, the total effect of advertising depends on the instantaneous effect plus any carryover. If the carryover is substantial, then ignoring this component can grossly underestimate the true effect of advertising. Second, if a pulse of advertising has some carryover effect, it may suggest that the next pulse need not be scheduled until the effect of first pulse decays. Third, the duration of the effects of advertising may have implications for whether firms should treat advertising as an expense or an investment and whether the government should allow it to be tax deductible or not.

A large number of primary econometric studies have attempted to estimate the size and duration of the carryover effect of advertising. We have two meta-analyses of these primary studies. This section summarizes what we have learned about advertising carryover from the two meta-analyses and from four important primary studies after these meta-analyses.

CLARKE (1976)

A marketing professor, Darral Clarke, carried out a meta-analysis of the carryover effect of advertising on sales or market share.[1] His study was pioneering in two ways. It was the first to review the past studies on the effects of advertising. It was the first to use a meta-analytic approach, even though he did not call it by that name. Clarke surveyed the results of 28 primary studies that analyzed the effects of advertising on sales or market share. From those, he found 69 estimates of the carryover effects of advertising. He then analyzed those estimates.

Clarke found that these estimates varied a great deal. As a result, they gave widely different estimates of how long it took for most (90%) of advertising's effects to last or dissipate. Estimates varied from a low of .8 of a month to a high of 1,368 months, or 113 years! On closer analysis, he found that a key factor affecting the estimates of the duration of advertising carryover was the level of *data aggregation.* This term refers to the level at which data on sales and advertising are collected and analyzed. In the sample of original studies Clarke surveyed, this aggregation could be in weeks, months, quarters, or years. He found that the higher the data aggregation, the longer the estimated duration of advertising's carryover (see Exhibit 7.1).

The challenge for Clarke was to come up with a criterion to indicate what would be the appropriate or "correct" data interval. He assumed that the appropriate data interval was the *purchase frequency*—the average frequency with which consumers purchase the product being studied. Based on that, he estimated that the duration of the effects of advertising on sales for the sample of categories he surveyed was between 3 and 15 months. He expected it to be definitely less than a year.

Clarke's study is pioneering in method and results. His major premise, that the duration of advertising's effects is less than 1 year, is still valid. However, his major assumption is probably not warranted—the appropriate data interval is the purchase frequency. Subsequent analysis suggests a lower more appropriate and much shorter duration interval. Thus, the duration of advertising's effects would probably be much shorter than that estimated by Clarke.

LEONE (1995)

A marketing professor, Robert Leone, computed the duration of the carryover effect from past studies.[2] In particular, he used as input the 114 estimates of the carryover effect of advertising collected by Assmus, Farley, and Lehmann (1984; see Chapter 6). To compute the duration of the carryover effect, Leone used the principle established by Clarke. Leone found that the average carryover effect of advertising was .69. Based on this figure, he found

Data Aggregation	Duration Interval in Months for 90% of Advertising's Total Effects
Weekly	0.9
Monthly	3.0
Bimonthly	9.0
Quarterly	25.1
Annually	56.5

Exhibit 7.1   Effects of Data Aggregation on Estimated Duration of Advertising's Effects

SOURCE: Adapted from Clarke (1976), "Econometric Measurement of the Duration of Advertising on Sales," *Journal of Marketing Research*, 13 (November), 345-357.

that 90% of the effect of advertising would last 6 months. This time period is a little shorter than that determined by Clarke, and is based on a large sample of primary studies.

TELLIS, CHANDY, AND THAIVANICH (2000)

Market experiments (also called field experiments) like the ones reviewed in Chapter 6 suggest that changes in the ad medium and creative are probably more effective than changes in the advertising budget. Past econometric studies had never addressed this issue in depth. In particular, managers need to know *which ads work, when, where, and how often.* Two of my associates and I conducted a study that tried to answer this question. The study used a model of advertising response at a highly disaggregate level of hours in the day when advertising occurred and consumers called back.[3]

We studied the television advertising of a firm that provides a referral service for consumers seeking a medical service. Consumers who respond to the ad are referred to an appropriate medical service provider. The latter pay the firm a fixed monthly fee for a minimum number of referrals per month. We modeled the advertising response for the firm at the hourly level and used a distributed lag model. A key feature of the model is that it captured the effects of individual ads, channels, and time of day. Data for the empirical testing were gathered for five markets in the United States.

We took pains to separate out the baseline referrals that were due to inherent characteristics of consumers and markets, from those which occurred in response to advertising. We found that baseline referrals during the day tend to follow a bell-shaped curve with the peak occurring in mid-morning. The numbers of calls made to the referral service were also not constant over the week, showing a declining trend as the week progressed.

One important aspect of the study was an analysis of advertising dynamics. As did many previous studies, we found that consumer response to an ad is not instantaneous but carries over to subsequent time periods. However, in contrast to most past studies, we found that the carryover effect of advertising was fairly short. Over the five markets studied, the average carryover effect was 8 hours (see Exhibit 7.2). A unique feature of this study was that the data were maintained and analyzed at the hourly level. Thus, consistent with the finding of Clarke (1976) that the duration of the carryover effect declines as the data get more disaggregate, we found that the carryover in our sample was quite short—just hours. This result reinforces the importance of testing advertising's carryover effect at a disaggregate level.

Another important result of the study was the finding that advertising carryover varied across cities and across times of the day. For example, there is a slight delay in the response to advertising, especially in the mornings, when consumers are very busy. This variation over time of the day and cities suggests that managers need to carry out their analyses by specific markets and time periods.

MELA, GUPTA, AND LEHMANN (1995)

Three marketing professors, Carl Mela, Sunil Gupta, and Donald Lehmann, examined the "long-term" effects of promotion and advertising on consumers' brand choice.[4] This study is probably one that focused on the longest time horizon—8¼ years. As such, the title of "long-term" is probably justified. The authors analyzed single-source data in one product category—a frequently purchased nonfood packaged product. During the time period of the study, the authors found that advertising had declined while promotions had increased.

The authors found that they could divide the market into two segments: a price-sensitive segment and a loyal segment. To analyze dynamics, they then divided the entire time period into quarterly periods. The authors found that the price-sensitive segment had grown over time. Furthermore, the consumers in the price-sensitive segment had become *more* price and promotion sensitive over time. That is, these consumers would respond more strongly to the same changes in price and promotions than they would in earlier time periods.

The authors' most important finding was the following. Over quarterly time periods, advertising reduces consumers' price sensitivity while promotion

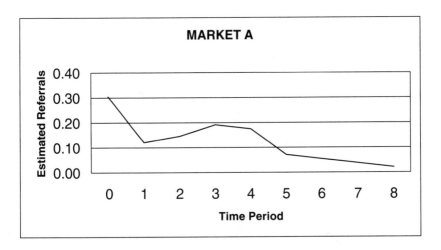

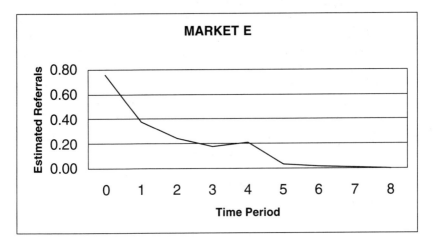

Exhibit 7.2   Advertising Carryover in Two Cities

SOURCE: Tellis, Gerard J., Rajesh Chandy, and Pattana Thaivanich (2000), "Decomposing the Effects of Direct Advertising: Which Brand Works, When, Where, and How Long?" *Journal of Marketing Research*, 37 (February), 32-46.

increases consumers' price and promotion sensitivity. They found that these effects were significantly larger for the price-sensitive segment than for the loyal segment. Note that the authors did not report any primary effects of advertising on consumers' choices or the market shares of brands. In other words, the only effects of advertising that they found were indirect effects on consumers' price and promotion sensitivity. Despite the changes they found, they did not observe any long-term changes in market share. That is, since all firms behaved similarly, they competed away any advantages or disadvantages from adopting such strategies.

However, to the extent that advertising made consumers less price sensitive, it had the potential of being more profitable. Subsequent analysis of profitability on the same data set indicated that advertising could be more profitable than promotions or price discounting.

INFORMATION RESOURCES, INC. EXPERIMENTS

These findings come from the study by Lodish and his associates at Information Resources, Inc. (IRI), which were reviewed in Chapter 6 of this book.[5] The readers should refer to that review to understand the background of the study.

The authors found that in general, the effects of advertising did not die out immediately after a campaign stopped. When advertising was effective, 76% of the initial increase persisted for a year later, *after the campaign ended,* and another 28% persisting for a third year. So the total carryover effect could equal the current effect (computed in the first year). In these cases, there was also a small (about 6%) carryover effect in category volume. Advertising effectiveness was also more persistent over time for new products than for mature products.

Note that the findings of this study seem to conflict sharply with those of Clarke (1976), who found that advertising carryover is from 3 to 9 months, and those of Tellis, Chandy, and Thaivanich (2000), who found that advertising carryover last only about 8 hours. One solution to this conflict comes from considering the time frame. Lodish et al.'s finding about advertising carryover is different from that computed in all prior studies reviewed above. The prior studies tried to estimate the average carryover effects of advertising in separate time periods or separate ads while the campaign is progressing. In contrast, Lodish and his associates estimated the carryover effect of an *entire campaign after it ended.* Thus, even though many authors have tried to compare the two types of findings and draw generalization, no simple comparison is valid. The two sets of findings must be treated as complementary findings about the carryover effects of advertising.

DEKIMPE AND HANSSENS (1995)

Marketing professors Marnik Dekimpe and Dominique Hanssens sought to determine the long-term or persistent impact of advertising.[6] They intentionally used a model different from that used by Clarke (1976) and all the studies reviewed above. They also sought to investigate a slightly different effect of advertising. They researched whether advertising could have some long-term effect that lasts even when the advertising is suspended. To do this analysis, the authors first carried out what is known as a *unit root test*. This test ascertains whether sales are stable or evolving over time. If the latter, the authors used their model to determine how strong the evolution is and whether advertising is responsible for the trend. They tested their model on monthly sales of a chain of home improvement stores from 1980 to 1986.

The authors found that sales and total advertising spending have a long-run or evolving component. The authors proposed that advertising has this effect for two reasons: repeat purchases from those who bought due to advertising and word-of-mouth effects of those who bought after hearing about the product from those who saw the advertising. They argued that these higher sales feed back into higher advertising as managers set ad budgets based on sales figures. They thus suspected that the evolving pattern they found was due to such a chain reaction.

The authors' most important and ambitious claim was that while some of the effect of advertising dissipates in the short term, some of it lasts or persists, even when the advertising is stopped. This *persistent* effect has also been called *hysterisis*. The authors did not give any time limit for this persistent effect. However, they did measure its size. They estimated that an extra dollar in advertising updates the long-run sales forecast by $1.09 and the long-run advertising forecast by $0.49. On the other hand, the authors found that even though advertising has a positive persistent effect, it does not have a positive persistent profit impact.

Such a persistent effect of advertising is unusual and unlikely to be general. Indeed, the authors did not claim that this effect applies for all products. However, they did emphasize that researchers need to test if such an effect is present in the advertising that they analyze.

Findings About Advertising Wearin and Wearout

Wearin and wearout are phenomena that refer to ad campaigns. Strictly speaking, a *campaign* is a series of ad exposures during a particular time period. The campaign could use just one ad or a series of differing ads so long as they have a common theme. A good recent example is the various executions of the MasterCard "There are some things money can't buy . . ." campaign, which ran successfully for more than 5 years.[7]

Wearin is the increasing response to an ad with increasing repetition of exposures of the ad (see Exhibit 1.2 in Chapter 1). This effect typically happens in the early stages of a campaign. In contrast, *wearout* refers to the decreasing response to an ad with increasing repetition of exposures of the ad. This effect typically occurs in the latter part of a campaign (see Exhibit 1.2). Thus, by their very definitions, the phenomena of wearin and wearout typically refer to the effectiveness of an ad campaign. Two reviews of the literature and three studies address the wearin and wearout of ad campaigns.

GREENBERG AND SUTTON (1973)

Two advertising researchers, Allan Greenberg and Charles Sutton, carried out an early, important review of published studies on wearout.[8] Most of their review focused on market studies, or quasi-market studies. Their review suggests the following major conclusions. Most of these conclusions are quite intuitive, so this chapter does not discuss the rationale for them.

- All ad campaigns ultimately wear out.
- Wearout refers only to ad campaigns that have had some positive effect. Ineffective campaigns cannot wear out.
- More effective campaigns might take longer to wear out than those that are less effective.
- A creative may wear out more slowly for product categories where purchase occurs infrequently than for those where it occurs frequently.
- Wearout occurs more slowly for campaigns in which exposures are spaced apart than for those in which they are positioned together.
- If a worn-out creative is reintroduced after a break, it might be effective once more. However, it will wear out even faster a second time around.
- Wearout of an ad campaign occurs faster among heavy TV viewers than among light TV viewers, assuming that the heavy TV viewers see the campaign more often than the light viewers.
- A creative that is simple or unambiguous wears out faster than one that is more complex or ambiguous. At the extreme, a creative that involves only a single punch line or point of humor wears out relatively fast.
- The use of a variety of creative executions in an ad campaign can delay wearout. Wearout is further delayed the more these individual executions differ from each other. In contrast, campaigns with just a single creative wear out relatively fast.

PECHMANN AND STEWART (1992)

Two marketing professors, Cornelia Pechmann and David Stewart, carefully reviewed all studies that included wearin and wearout.[9] None of their conclusions contradict those of Greenberg and Sutton. However, some of their conclusions complement those of the previous review, especially on wearout. Here are their main conclusions:

- Wearin either does not exist or occurs quite rapidly. That is, if an ad is going to be effective, it will be so early rather than late in the campaign.
- Wearin may take a little longer in the field than it does in the laboratory. The reason is that in the field all consumers may not see an ad every time it is released. In addition, even if they do see the ad, consumers' exposure in the field tends to be voluntary, while that in the laboratory tends to be forced.
- Wearin may also occur more slowly when ads are scheduled apart rather than when they are scheduled together.
- Ads that use emotional appeals wear out more slowly than those that use arguments.
- Wearin and wearout occur faster for consumers who are highly motivated and actively process the message in the ads than for those consumers who are not so motivated and active.

TELLIS, CHANDY, AND THAIVANICH (2000)

The study by Tellis, Chandy, and Thaivanich,[10] reviewed earlier, also examined the wearin and wearout of the creative. The advertiser in that study retained all its old creative executions, which it used in old and new markets. Thus, the authors had access to a bank of more than 60 creative executions, which were aired over a variety of cities, time periods, and durations. Indeed, this study is probably the largest field study that rigorously examined the wearin and wearout of ads. Here are the main conclusions:

- Behavioral response of a creative declined steadily with use.
- The strongest response occurred in the first week in which the creative was aired. That is, wearin is immediate.
- Wearout occurred from the second week of use of a creative. That is, wearout starts quite early in the life of a creative.
- Wearout is steepest in the first few weeks of the airing of a creative (see Exhibit 7.3).

Thus, consistent with the results of Jones (1995; see Chapter 6) and others, ads did not seem to have much of a wearin. On the contrary, they began to wear out soon after being used, and the wearout was fairly rapid early on in its use.

HENDERSON BLAIR (2000)

Margaret Henderson Blair, an advertising researcher, analyzed the effects of 20 split-cable copy tests for wearin and wearout.[11] She measured response in terms of awareness and trial. She is one of the few authors to report substantial wearin. Her major findings are the following:

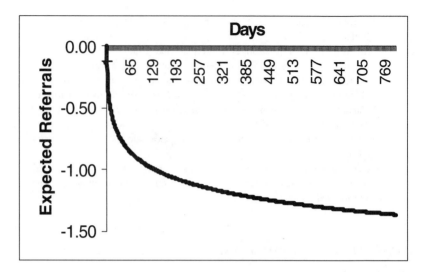

Exhibit 7.3   Average Wearout in Effectiveness of Individual Ads

SOURCE: Adapted fromTellis, Gerard J., Rajesh Chandy, and Pattana Thaivanich (2000), "Decomposing the Effects of Direct Advertising: Which Brand Works, When, Where, and How Long?" *Journal of Marketing Research*, 37 (February), 32-46.

NOTE: Response is in decline referrals from peak response. Time is in days from first airing of ad.

- Ads show both wearin and wearout.
- Ads with higher persuasion scores show stronger wearin with increasing delivery of gross ratings points (GRPs) in the market than those with lower persuasion scores.
- Totally ineffective ads show neither wearin nor wearout.

OTHER STUDIES

Some other studies found other complementary results about wearin and wearout.

- An article reported on 168 studies involving 58 product categories and 111 brands in five countries of North America and Europe.[12] The results suggest that wearout does occur internationally, as in the Henderson Blair study above.
- A recent study about attention suggests no wearin and immediate wearout as in the Tellis et al. study above.[13] The study found that attention to an ad decreased almost 50% from the first to the third repetition, in both natural and artificial conditions. The immediate decline in attention with repetition may be one reason for the early wearout of the creatives.

Findings About Advertising Content

An emerging stream of research in market studies is to determine the effectiveness of individual ads and their content on sales and market share. There are only two major studies in this stream of research.

CHANDY, TELLIS, MacINNIS, AND THAIVANICH (2001)

As this and the previous chapter indicate, there are a vast number of market studies on advertising effectiveness. Almost all of these studies have focused on either advertising weight, elasticity, or frequency. None of these studies has considered the role of individual ads and especially the content or creative of these ads. In contrast, a vast literature in consumer behavior has addressed how the content of an ad must be configured to make the ad effective. However, most of these studies have been laboratory experiments conducted in highly artificial environments.

A unique study by Chandy, Tellis, MacInnis, and Thaivanich tried to integrate these two streams of research.[14] We sought to determine the effectiveness of various ad appeals in real-market situations. Our study was an extension of the one reported above for the referral service. The service started initially in only one city (market). Over a decade, it gradually expanded to cover more than 23 markets. Thus, the markets varied in age from a few months to more than 10 years. During that time, the service developed a set of 72 ads that it used with varying frequency and intensity over the various cities.

One important finding was that the effects of advertising on sales and profits varied substantially over markets, TV channels, and especially creatives. Many creative executions were not effective in increasing sales, and most were not profitable. A valuable part of the analysis was its specific findings about creative executions, media, and time slots that worked. The analysis pinpointed which creative executions the advertiser should pursue and those it should drop, the channels it should use and those it should drop, and the time slots in which media buys would be most productive.

The ads themselves used a variety of appeals. We measured these appeals on a rich set of behavioral variables. In particular, we assessed to what extent the ads used argument, emotion, or endorsement; how the message was framed; and how long the key message was on. With these measures, we were able to assess the effectiveness of various ad appeals depending on whether they were used in new versus old markets. A general finding was that advertising response was stronger in younger markets.

The results of the study indicate that argument-based appeals, expert sources, and negatively framed messages are particularly effective in new markets. Emotion-based appeals and positively framed messages are more effective in old markets. These results suggest that ads should be tailored to fit the age of specific markets, with different ads for different ages.

MacINNIS, RAO, AND WEISS (2002)

Three marketing professors, Deborah MacInnis, Ambar Rao, and Allen Weiss, reported on a set of multistage experiments conducted in the 1990s.[15] The authors developed a database of TV commercials that had been used in advertising weight tests for frequently purchased products, such as those reported in the IRI and Campbell Soup experiments discussed in Chapter 6. The database contained 47 ads, each tested in a different market experiment. Twenty-five of these ads produced statistically significant increases in sales, and 22 did not.

The authors then recruited and trained a set of 22 paid judges to evaluate these ads on a scale. The scale characterized the ads as primarily emotional, rational, or heuristic based. Emotional ads work by arousing the feelings of viewers. Rational ads work by appealing to their logic. Heuristic-based ads work by inducing viewers to make inferences about the advertised brand. The authors expected emotional ads to do better in weight tests for these mature, frequently purchased product categories. The reason is that consumers are well informed about the brands and so would not respond to higher levels of rational appeals. At the same time, they had little motivation to process advertising information. So they would be more likely to respond to emotional appeals that engaged their feelings.

The results show that emotional ads were significantly more likely to have produced increases in sales in the weight tests. On the other hand, ads that used heuristic-based or rational appeals were more likely to have not produced increases in sales in the weight tests. In a further experiment, the authors pursued whether these ads affected subjects in laboratory conditions. They found that ads that produced positive feeling and limited negative feelings were more likely to have produced increases in sales in the weight tests.

The message from these experiments is that in frequently purchased mature product categories, emotional ads that create positive feelings and limit negative feelings can benefit from increased advertising.

Summary

This section summarizes the findings about market effects of advertising carryover, wearin and wearout, and advertising content.

FINDINGS ABOUT ADVERTISING CARRYOVER

The following effects of advertising were very general:

- The effects of advertising are noninstantaneous. That is, advertising has some carryover effect.
- Advertising's carryover needs to be modeled very carefully with appropriate data. The estimated duration of advertising's carryover increases with the level of data aggregation. In particular, two contrasting recent studies show the following:

    In terms of total weight of a 1-year ad campaign, advertising carryover may last as long as another 2 years.

    In terms of individual ads analyzed in very small time periods such as hours, advertising carryover may be quite short, lasting just about 8 hours.

The following effects are important although they have been confirmed by only one study:

- Advertising seems to have some indirect, long-term positive brand effect in terms of reducing consumers' price and promotion sensitivity.
- In some situations, advertising shows some hysterisis. That is, it can cause some permanent or persistent increase in sales.
- Within a product category, advertising carryover of the same ad varies some-what across cities and across time of day.

FINDINGS ABOUT WEARIN

- Wearin either does not exist or occurs quite rapidly.
- Wearin occurs more slowly:

    When exposures are schedule apart

    When attention is not forced

    For emotional appeals relative to arguments

    For consumers who are not highly motivated or active in processing ad messages

    In field situations relative to laboratory settings

- Wearin might be stronger with ads that have higher persuasion scores.

FINDINGS ABOUT WEAROUT

- All ad campaigns ultimately wear out.
- Wearout may occur more slowly:

For a creative that is complex, uses an emotional appeal, or is ambiguous

For ads that are less effective than those that are more effective

For product categories where purchase occurs infrequently than for those where it occurs frequently

For campaigns in which exposures are scheduled apart than for those in which they are scheduled together

For light viewers of TV than for heavy viewers

For campaigns that use a variety of creative executions relative to those that use a single creative

- If a worn-out creative is reintroduced after a break, it might be effective once more. However, it will wear out even faster a second time around.

FINDINGS ABOUT CONTENT

- Changes in the creative, medium, target segment, or product itself sometimes lead to changes in sales, even though an increase in the level of advertising by itself does not.

Notes

1.   Clarke, Darral G. (1976), "Econometric Measurement of the Duration of Advertising Effect on Sales," *Journal of Marketing Research,* 13 (November), 345-357.

2.   Leone, Robert P. (1995), "Generalizing What Is Known About Temporal Aggregation and Advertising Carryover," *Marketing Science,* 14, 3, Part 2 of 2, G141-G149.

3.   Tellis, Gerard J., Rajesh Chandy, and Pattana Thaivanich (2000), "Decomposing the Effects of Direct Advertising: Which Brand Works, When, Where, and How Long?" *Journal of Marketing Research,* 37 (February), 32-46.

4.   Mela, Carl F., Sunil Gupta, and Donald R. Lehmann (1997), "The Long-Term Impact of Promotion and Advertising on Consumer Brand Choice," *Journal of Marketing Research,* 34 (May), 248-261. See also Jedidi, Kamel, Carl F. Mela, and Sunil Gupta (1999), "Managing Advertising and Promotion for Long-Run Profitability," *Marketing Science,* 18, 1, 1-22.

5.   Lodish, Leonard M., et al. (1995), "How T.V. Advertising Works: A Meta-Analysis of 389 Real World Split Cable T.V. Advertising," *Journal of Marketing Research,* 32 (May), 125-139; Lodish, Leonard M., et al (1995), "A Summary of Fifty-Five In-Market Experimental Estimates of the Long-Term Effect of TV Advertising," *Marketing Science,* 14, 3, Part 2 of 2, G133-G139.

6.   Dekimpe, Marnik G., and Dominique M. Hanssens (1995), "The Persistence of Marketing Effects on Sales," *Marketing Science,* 14, 1, 1-21.

7.   O'Connell, Vanessa (2002), "MasterCard 'Priceless' Ads Grow Old—Campaign Lifted Company at Its Onset Five Years Ago, but Rivals Grab Attention," *Wall Street Journal,* September 30.

8.   Greenberg, Allan, and Charles Sutton (1973), "Television Commercial Wearout," *Journal of Advertising Research,* 13 (October), 47-54.

9.   Pechmann, Cornelia, and David W. Stewart (1992), "Advertising Repetition: A Critical Review of Wearin and Wearout," *Current Issues and Research in Advertising,* 11, 2, 285-330; Sawyer, Alan (1981), "Repetition, Cognitive Responses and Persuasion," in *Cognitive Responses in*

Persuasion, Richard E. Petty, Thomas M. Ostrom, and Timothy C. Brock (eds.), Hillsdale, NJ: Lawrence Erlbaum; Sawyer, Alan, and Scott Ward (1976), *Carry-Over Effects in Advertising Communication: Evidence and Hypotheses From Behavioral Science*, Cambridge, MA: Marketing Science Institute.

10. Tellis et al., "Decomposing the Effects."

11. Henderson Blair, Margaret (2000), "An Empirical Investigation of Advertising Wearin and Wearout," *Journal of Advertising Research* (November/December), 95-100.

12. Masterson, Peggy (1999), "The Wearout Phenomenon," *Marketing Research*, 11, 3 (Fall), 26-31.

13. Pieters, Rik, Edward Rosbergen, and Michel Wedel (1999), "Visual Attention to Repeated Print Advertising: A Test of Scanpath Theory," *Journal of Marketing Research*, 36, 4 (November), 424-438.

14. Rajesh Chandy, Gerard J. Tellis, Debbie MacInnis, and Pattana Thaivanich (2001), "What to Say When: Advertising Appeals in Evolving Markets," *Journal of Marketing Research*, 38, 4 (November), 399-414.

15. MacInnis, Deborah, Ambar G. Rao, and Allen M. Weiss (2002), "Assessing When Increased Media Weight Helps Sales of Real World Brands," *Journal of Marketing Research*, 39 (November), 391-407.

Part III

*Findings From Experimental
Studies: How and Why
Advertising Works*

8

Advertising as Persuasion

The previous chapters emphasized how changes in the weight of advertising alone were insufficient to increase sales and market share. On the other hand, changes in the content of ads were a primary means of increasing their effectiveness. Unfortunately, there are only a few market studies about how such changes affect the sales or market share of a brand. However, a wealth of laboratory studies do show how advertising, especially its content, persuades consumers. Most of these studies rely on experiments or theater tests (see Chapter 5). These have occurred in diverse fields such as psychology, communication, marketing, consumer behavior, and advertising. Because such research has not been tested in real markets, the results need to be treated with some caution. Nevertheless, in the absence of field studies, this body of research remains the best means of understanding how and why advertising works.

This body of research also provides a rich source of principles for designing ad content. In contrast to the prevailing view in the field, being different, or resorting to lateral, divergent, or illogical thinking, is neither the sole nor sufficient condition for developing effective creatives. Rather, the body of research provides numerous norms and rules of which types of ad content are effective in which contexts. Thus, they can constitute various templates for creativity.[1] Also, the rules, norms, or templates are not necessarily disjointed. Rather, they can be integrated into a whole or theory. Such a theory is easy to absorb and remember and also provides a parsimonious explanation.

This chapter and Chapters 9, 10, and 11 review this body of research about how and why advertising works. This chapter provides an overview of how advertising persuades consumers to act. It delineates three unique forms of persuasion: argument, emotion, and endorsement. The subsequent three chapters address each of these topics. This chapter focuses on broad principles of persuasion such as the routes of persuasion, low-involvement persuasion, and the role of repetition in persuasion. The attempt throughout these four chapters is to present findings in the context of an integrated framework or theory.

Routes of Persuasion

This chapter defines *ad persuasion* as a change in opinion, attitude, or behavior due to ad exposure. This definition is purposely broad, as it does not specify the type of communication by which the change occurs.

Many people assume that persuasion involves the use of information and argument. Indeed, this is an important means of persuasion and is the definition of persuasion that the dictionary adopts. Our definition of persuasion includes change that is brought about either by reason or by other subtler means that do not involve any reasoning. Examples of the latter include the use of cues, such as endorsers, and that of emotion, such as fear or joy.

There are numerous routes by which an ad can persuade consumers.[2] Moreover, because persuasion is a pervasive phenomenon in all walks of life, researchers have proposed many theories to explain each of these routes. Indeed, the literature on how advertising persuades is so vast that one chapter cannot do justice to it all. What we need is a simple framework that parsimoniously summarizes all the various routes of persuasion and succinctly explains the reasons for each.

Fortunately, we do have such a framework, albeit it has the unwieldy name of the *elaboration likelihood model*. More simply, this term refers to how likely a person is to think deeply (elaborate) about an ad, when exposed to it. Two psychologists, John Cacioppo and Richard Petty, developed this framework and have amassed a great deal of empirical support in its favor.[3] This chapter presents a modified version of the framework, which can serve to organize all modes of persuasion and all types of appeals.

CHOICE OF ROUTES

The basic premise of this model is that the route by which an ad persuades consumers depends on how much they think about the ad's message. When people have both the motivation and the ability to evaluate a message, their likelihood of thinking about it will be high. They will look for and respond to strong arguments in favor of the message and counter what they think are weak reasons. This route of potential persuasion is called the central route. Chapter 9 discusses in depth the use of arguments in ads to persuade consumers.

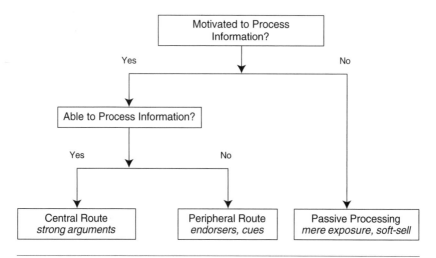

Exhibit 8.1   Modified Elaboration Likelihood Model

SOURCE: Adapted from Cacioppo, John T., and Richard E. Petty (1985), "Central and Peripheral Routes to Persuasion: The Role of Message Repetition," in Linda F. Alwitt and Andrew A. Mitchell (eds.), *Psychological Processes and Advertising Effects: Theory, Research and Applications,* Hillsdale, NJ: Lawrence Erlbaum, 90-111.

If consumers have the motivation but lack the ability to evaluate a message, they are likely to respond to cues associated with the message (see Exhibit 8.1). This form of persuasion is called the peripheral route.

Examples of persuasion cues are the presence of an endorser, the fame of an endorser, the glamour of the medium, the costliness of the ad, flowery copy, or the number of arguments in the ad (as opposed to the strength of the arguments). For example, during the height of the Internet boom in 2000, Internet firms accounted for 1% of the total advertising spending in the economy but 33% of that spent during the Super Bowl. The Super Bowl is an expensive medium that firms use as much to signal their standards as to target a particular audience. Thus, these Internet firms were probably hoping to impress on consumers and investors that they were viable. Nevertheless, the most common cue used by advertisers is endorsers. Chapter 11 discusses in depth the use of endorsers in ads to persuade consumers.

If people lack both the motivation and the ability to process the message in an ad, they are in a passive state of receptivity to an ad, if at all they attend to it. This state of ad receptivity has also been called low-involvement processing. In this situation, they are likely to respond to humor and drama (see Exhibit 8.1). Thus, people are "neither always thoughtful nor always mindless" in forming

Copy of Ad Using Strong Argument Scientifically Designed	Copy of Ad Using Weak Argument Designed for Beauty
New advanced honing method creates unsurpassed sharpness	Floats in water with a minimum of rust
Special chemically formulated coating eliminates nicks and cuts and prevents rusting	Comes in various sizes, shapes, and colors
Handle is tapered and ribbed to prevent slipping	Designed with the bathroom in mind
In direct comparison tests the Edge blade gave twice as many close shaves as its nearest competitor	
Unique angle placement of the blade provides the smoothest shave possible	Can only be used once but will be memorable

Exhibit 8.2   Alternate Copy of Ads for Fictitious Edge Disposable Razor

SOURCE: Petty, Richard E. and John T. Cacioppo and David Schumann (1983), "Central and Peripheral Routes to Advertising Effectiveness: The Moderating Role of Involvement," *Journal of Consumer Research*, 10 September, 135-146. Reprinted with the permission of the University of Chicago Press.

their opinions and decisions, but are likely to adopt a central, peripheral, or passive route to persuasion depending on their motivation and ability.[4] Note that both motivation and ability are required for the central route.

Motivation is the willingness of the individual to evaluate a message. Motivation may be due to the importance of the advertised item, the loyalty to the advertised brand, or a very engaging ad. Ability is the competence of the individual to engage in the required mental effort. Ability requires adequate language skills, proper training in logical thinking, adequate knowledge about the issues, and time and quiet to carefully think through the issues.

One study that nicely shows the two routes of persuasion is a laboratory experiment with a fictitious "Edge" brand of disposable razors.[5] The ads used either strong arguments or weak arguments (see Exhibit 8.2) and were endorsed either by famous athletes or the lay public. In addition, the researchers manipulated subjects to fall into two conditions of involvement in the message of the ad. The results of the study demonstrate that when subjects are involved with the message, a central route of processing is more effective.

In this case, the strength of the argument is important for effective persuasion (see top panel Exhibit 8.3). But when subjects are not involved with the message, a peripheral route of processing may be effective. In this case, cues such as

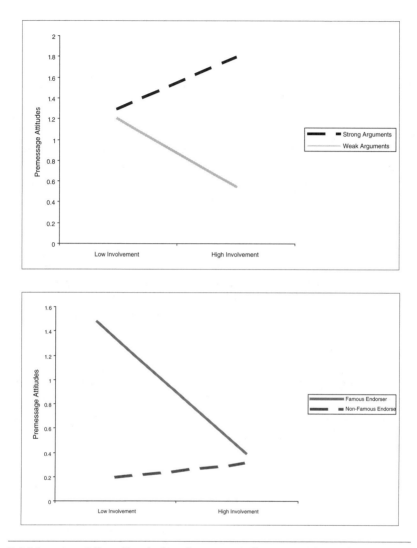

Exhibit 8.3   Effect of Level of Involvement on Effectiveness of Appeals

SOURCE: Adapted from Petty, Richard E., John T. Cacioppo, and David Schumann (1983), "Central and Peripheral Routes to Advertising Effectiveness: The Moderating Role of Involvement," *Journal of Consumer Research*, 10 (September), 135-146. Reprinted with permission of the University of Chicago Press.

the type of endorser are important for effective persuasion (see bottom panel of Exhibit 8.3). Another study finds that the strength of argument is also important when the message is inconsistent with the receiver's prevailing preferences. In such a scenario, a strong argument is more persuasive than a weak argument.

STABILITY OF PERSUASION

How does persuasion differ by these different routes? In particular, which one lasts longer, and which is easier to achieve? This section addresses this issue. Research has compared persuasion by the central and peripheral routes in terms of permanence of the change and the resistance to change.

Permanence is the extent to which the change caused by persuasion endures. Changes that occur via the central route are generally thought to be more permanent than those that occur via the peripheral route. The reason is that individuals who use the central route engage in careful and detailed analysis of the arguments, comparing them against their own prior views and arriving at some well-worked-out conclusion. These individuals are likely to remember the issues or at least the conclusion because of the effort involved, and they hold to the changed opinion or attitude. On the other hand, because the peripheral route involves simple inferences based on persuasion cues, the issues and conclusions are unlikely to be remembered for long. Permanence can be enhanced to some extent by the use of cues that are related to the brand and the message.[6]

Repetition is more likely to be effective for the peripheral route than for the central route. For the central route, the repetition of the strong arguments may lead to tedium and irritation, unless the arguments are suitably complex.

Resistance is the extent to which the changes due to persuasion survive attacks based on new information. Although permanence is likely to occur with resistance, the two concepts are independent as can be seen from cultural truisms.[7] Belief in a truism such as "brush your teeth every morning on waking up to avoid cavities" is generally instilled more by repetition in childhood, reinforced by the authority of adults, than by careful arguments. Individuals who do not develop these beliefs by arguments have a hard time defending them. Cultural truisms unsupported by arguments may be permanent, but are not resistant.

Persuasion by the central route is usually permanent and resistant. Persuasion by the peripheral route is neither permanent nor resistant. However, it can be made more enduring by repetition, and made more resistant by the provision of supporting arguments. For example, until 25 years ago, the dominance of Coca-Cola in the United States may have been due to consumers' loyalty to the brand developed over generations, passed on through family behavior, and reinforced by ads that use the peripheral route of persuasion. In the 1970s, Pepsi attacked the position of Coca-Cola using arguments in ads that showed consumers prefer Pepsi in blind taste tests. Drinkers of Coca-Cola had weak defenses against this frontal attack. The advertising strategy was effective, leading to greater parity in the market shares of the two brands.

Low-Involvement or Passive Processing

Much television advertising today contains numerous repetitions of short commercials that offer only limited information and seem trivial or sometimes plain silly. Journalists sometimes comment on the emptiness of these ads, while social critics decry their shallowness. Many critics of advertising suggest that the low level of attention that consumers pay to television ads may cause them to be ineffective. Yet some advertisers affirm their faith in such ads by spending billions of dollars on them each year.

Herbert Krugman was one of the first to make a convincing case for the effectiveness of the apparently simplistic ad.[8] He suggested that communication through TV ads is different from that which takes place through ads in newspapers or brochures, which tend to have extensive copy and strong arguments. The difference is due to the involvement of the audience. Krugman claimed that much television advertising receives low-involvement processing in which consumers notice the ads but do not process or think about them extensively. He argued that repetition of such ads could persuade as effectively, if not more so, than that which occurred through the repetition of ads with strong arguments. Indeed, the distracted state in which consumers view these ads may lead to a lowering of the consumers' defenses and an easier acceptance of the message.

Krugman's ideas have spawned a whole stream of research on the role of low-involvement processing.[9] This research has expanded the concept and enriched the explanation of the phenomenon. The term *involvement* as used here primarily refers to cognitive involvement, where the receiver of a message may engage in more or less active processing of the message. An individual's level of involvement may arise due to several factors. In general, the elaboration likelihood model suggests that motivation and ability determine whether a consumer falls in this state of low involvement.

Specifically, the context, message, individual, brand, or ad itself can influence whether a consumer is high or low involvement. The context of an ad is the program in which or the people with whom it is viewed. Contextual involvement could be triggered by a question in the ad that leads to a discussion with others watching the ad. Message involvement arises from an individual's immersion in important or controversial issues, symbols, or images that the ad raises. Individual involvement arises because of the individual's natural interest in the advertised product category. Brand involvement arises because of the individual's knowledge about the brand. The ad itself can trigger involvement when it breaks through the noise of competing ads and messages and grabs consumers' attention.[10] Low-involvement processing results when none of these factors lead the consumer to be involved in an ad.

Recent research supports Krugman's intuition about low-involvement processing and provides a rationale for the effect. For example, one study found that subjects were more likely to believe trivial statements when they were less involved in evaluating them.[11] The study argued that if subjects were involved in the statements they were more likely to evaluate the truth of the statements based on their knowledge and reasoning. But if they were distracted and not involved they were more likely to respond based on their familiarity with the statements formed from repetition. Indeed, less-involved subjects judged the information to be more believable when they experienced an "it rings a bell" reaction. These results show that persuasion by low involvement does take place, and it is enhanced by the subject's lack of involvement in the message.

Thus, distraction during advertising can be an asset if it reduces resistance to a message without lowering exposure to it. Advertisers need to know what factors distract consumers in this way.

The chapter next considers three specific appeals of low-involvement processing: mere exposure, priming, soft sell, and subliminal advertising.

MERE EXPOSURE[12]

Mere exposure suggests that the mere act of the repetitive exposure of a stimulus can lead to preference for it, even though consumers do not remember the exposure. For example, frequent listening to a song may lead to its preference over an unfamiliar song. Consumers' liking for certain jingles, slogans, and logos after repetitive exposure to them in ads may be due to this effect of repetition.

A psychologist, Robert Zajonc, stimulated much research in this field. A vast number of studies tried to replicate the findings of Zajonc under different conditions and with different stimuli. While the results are not identical, the cumulative evidence suggests that increasing repetition leads to increased liking for the stimuli. However, beyond some point of saturation, increasing repetition leads to decreased liking for the stimuli.[13] While the original research of Zajonc and others who followed him used meaningless symbols, repetitive exposure is likely to have even more impact for meaningful stimuli, such as brand names, taglines, and slogans.

Why does repetition lead to liking in this way? The two-factor theory of habituation and tedium, discussed below, could explain the effect.

Repetitive exposure is most important for new brands and products. For example, new candidates for minor elections often plaster a simple ad bearing their image and name on every available street corner and public building. Because of the vast number of candidates and posts, the public is unlikely to remember all the names or even to have heard of them. In that case, voters are going to be doubtful of such candidates and not vote for them. The candidate's goal is to increase exposure and repetition of the name so consumers do not find it strange. In general, consumers are unlikely to choose brands of which they have never previously heard. On the contrary, under uncertainty, consumers are likely to choose the brand they are most familiar with. This is especially true of important, expensive, or sensitive products. Thus, repetitive exposure to new brands in these contexts can be the first step to trial and purchase.

PRIMING

Priming is a phenomenon wherein exposure to a brand name during some entertaining or distracting event leads to better recall and preference for that name, even without recall of the exposure.[14]

For example, consider an experiment involving two groups of subjects, each exposed to a movie involving a hotel scene. One group sees the scene while in a Marriott hotel. The other group sees the identical scene, and the only change is that the hotel is Hilton. When asked to recall some brand names, the former group will recall Marriott with much higher probability than the latter group. Yet neither of those groups is likely to recall exposure to any ad.

Priming probably depends on the theory of implicit memory. Accordingly to this theory, individuals are able to recall certain events or activities without recalling the details associated with them. For example, we may know how to drive different types of cars spontaneously when sitting in them even though we may not be able to write out the exact steps to do so, when in a classroom.

Priming may explain the potential effectiveness of much contemporary advertising. A large number of ads that we see on TV, especially those containing humorous or entertaining dramas, seem to be unrelated to the brand and the message. However, to the extent that these ads obtain exposure for the advertised brand name, they may prime consumers to think of the brand at the time of decision making. Priming is also the major reason for advertiser choice of product placements. The latter are paid placements by a firm of its brand name in a movie, news item, or any regular programming in the media.

In contrast to mere exposure, priming is probably most advantageous for established or dominant brands. Such brands have already established a reputation in the market and are probably already familiar to consumers. Their need is to obtain top-of-mind awareness, so that when a consumer is about to make a decision, he or she thinks of the primed brand name, rather than any of the rivals.

SOFT-SELL MESSAGES

A soft-sell message is a subtle one that allows for different interpretations, persuades by suggestion, and makes no direct request for action or change. The ad for Guess apparel in Exhibit 8.4 is an example. Because of the expressiveness of the picture and the ambiguity of the message, repetition is likely to increase recall of the brand and positive feelings toward it. Repetition is unlikely to lead to tedium soon. Moreover, in the presence of favorable brand experience, a soft-sell message may induce a viewer to develop his or her own positive interpretation of the message, enhancing the effectiveness of the ad.[15] This effect is stronger in low-involvement than in high-involvement conditions, and also stronger for attributes the consumer must experience to understand, such as the taste of food.[16] In Bozell's campaign for milk, the milk mustache itself can be interpreted as a soft sell that is subject to different interpretations. For example, most consumers would find the ad funny; some consumers might evoke warm images of drinking milk as a kid; others might find their favorite celebrity looking cute with a milk mustache; still others might imply milk is cool.

The term *hard sell* is often used as the opposite of soft sell. Hard-sell messages are direct requests to act accompanied with some pressure or urgency. One example is the type of discount ad that some auto retailers often run, "Every car in the showroom on sale. Unbelievable discounts! Hurry. Visit our showroom while super deals last." Repetition is likely to lead to greater comfort with and acceptance of the soft-sell message, but to greater tedium and irritation with the hard-sell message.

SUBLIMINAL ADVERTISING

Subliminal advertising refers to persuasive ad messages that are just below the threshold of perception and are embedded in material that can be perceived. Examples would include messages flashed between images of a video ad so quickly that they cannot be seen, or messages that can be heard only when a tune is played backward. Proponents claim that subliminal messages work because these messages are perceived subconsciously while recipients are not conscious of them and thus cannot resist their influence.

Is mere exposure the same as subliminal advertising? Actually, subliminal advertising is quite different from mere exposure. Mere exposure assumes that stimuli are perceptible even if not intelligible, which become effective through repetition. Subliminal advertising assumes that the stimuli are intelligible even though they are not perceived normally. It is supposedly effective due to lack of awareness of or resistance to the ad.

The controversy about subliminal advertising started in the 1950s based on an experiment described in Vance Packard's best-seller, *Hidden*

Exhibit 8.4   A Soft-Sell Ad

SOURCE: Guess, Inc.

Persuaders.[17] In the experiment by James McDonald Vicary, the words "eat popcorn" and "drink Coca-Cola" were flashed on a screen for only 1/3000th of a second. The sales were supposed to have increased 58% for Coke and 18% for popcorn. If advertising could persuade people against their will and knowledge, it would be a truly strong force. Although a few researchers in the area still believe in subliminal advertising, the majority disbelieve in its effectiveness. Moreover, the effects are so debatable that even some proponents of the theory question its commercial viability.[18] The current thinking among professional psychologists and advertisers is that subliminal advertising is not effective for three reasons.

First, many attempts were made to replicate Vicary's study. Most failed to find any significant support for subliminal advertising.[19] Second, the original study itself did not have any strong control groups. Indeed, some researchers think the original study is seriously flawed if not actually fabricated. One recent review suggests that Vicary used his claims of the effectiveness of subliminal advertising to collect retainer and consulting fees from advertisers, and then in June 1958, he supposedly disappeared without a trace.[20] Third, the major argument against subliminal advertising is that it is difficult for something to be effective if it is not even perceived by the human senses.

Moreover, if subliminal messages were all that effective, government agencies could use subliminal advertising to cure social ills and criminal behavior, such as use of illicit drugs, child abuse, drunk driving, theft, and homicide.[21]

Nevertheless, the public continues to believe in subliminal advertising. Surveys have found that 40% to 50% of the public has heard of the term and that a majority of these people (70% to 80%) believe that advertisers use it.[22] This belief may reflect the public's general skepticism about advertisers, and it may be fueled by the uncritical accounts of the efficacy of subliminal advertising by attention-seeking journalists.

Repetition in Persuasion

Repetition is the exposure of an ad (or some other stimulus) to a subject two or more times in succession. Repetition is a major factor in advertising today. It is studied extensively in the fields of psychology, marketing, advertising, and consumer behavior.

For decades, advertising researchers have been searching for the holy grail of effective frequency, the precise number of exposures that maximizes consumer response to an ad. It has become the magical number that tells a manager how long to run a campaign, and thus how much to spend on advertising. The advertising literature on this topic can be divided into two schools of thought, minimalists and repetitionists.

Minimalists are those who believe that a few exposures achieve the maximum response. An early proponent of this view is advertising researcher

Herbert Krugman. He argued that three exposures were enough.[23] Another researcher, Colin McDonald, was one of the earliest to empirically test this hypothesis. He found that response peaked at two exposures[24] (see Chapter 6). A third researcher, Michael Naples, popularized these results with the concept of effective frequency.[25] These studies dominated debate on this issue for a long time because compelling empirical evidence was hard to come by. More recently, studies by John Philip Jones and Lawrence Gibson have rekindled the debate by arguing that the three exposures of Krugman and the two-exposure finding of McDonald may be too high[26] (see Chapter 6).

At the other end of this spectrum are repetitionists, those who believe that advertising repetition is essential for optimal consumer response. One of the earliest and most compelling studies supporting this view is that by an advertising researcher, Hubert Zielske.[27] He found that repetition of a message as many as 13 times continued to increase consumer response albeit at a declining rate, as measured by recall of the message. When these repetitions were massed over 13 weeks, that response peaked quickly but also decayed rapidly. However, when the repetitions were spaced out once a month over a year, the response continued to increase steadily during that period to reach a similar peak, but with much less decay (see Exhibit 8.5).

Other studies have also shown that some delay in the delivery of exposures can increase the probability of positive effects of repetition.[28] For example, a pattern of five exposures each delivered a day apart is better than one of five exposures all delivered on the same day.[29]

A large number of studies on message repetition have led to some consistent findings about its effects.[30]

Repetition leads to higher persuasion, measured by variables such as attention, recognition, recall, attitude, preference, behavioral intention, and behavior.

The positive effect of repetition on each of these variables declines roughly in the order listed, with the strongest effect on attention and the least strong on behavior.

Most important, the response to repetition is generally nonlinear, first increasing and then leveling off or declining.

Studies on wearin and wearout, reviewed in Chapter 7, also suggest that repetition of ads up to 15 exposures in 2 months has increasing returns. Thus, a considerable body of research suggests that the effects of advertising are not instantaneous but increase with repetition, at least in the first few months of a campaign. These findings contrast with the findings of minimalists.

Which of these two perspectives is right?

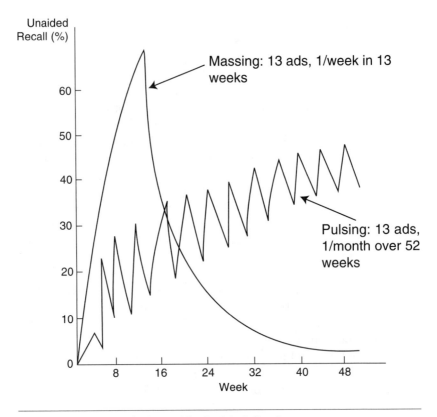

Exhibit 8.5   Effect of Ad Repetition by Scheduling Strategy

SOURCE: Adapted from Zielske, Hubert A. (1959), "The Remembering and Forgetting of Advertising," *Journal of Marketing*, 23, 1, 239-243. Reprinted with permission of the American Marketing Association.

FACTORS INFLUENCING REPETITION

Perhaps neither view is completely correct. Neither view constitutes a law or a universal generalization about advertising's effects. Either view may be right under certain conditions. Indeed, both these schools of thought may even be describing the same phenomenon. The reason they seem opposed is that each view refers to a different context of advertising and response. The context of advertising is what determines whether one, two, or many exposures are necessary for optimal sales. This context of advertising can be defined in terms of brand familiarity, message novelty, and message complexity. These three factors constitute the key elements of a theory of repetition and effective frequency.

Brand Familiarity

Brand familiarity refers to consumers' knowledge of, experience with, or loyalty to the advertised brand. Familiarity may be the most important factor that moderates effective frequency. It may also be the underlying factor in some brand-related variables such as the brand's market share, newness, or order of entry into the market. Thus, by focusing on one underlying factor, familiarity, we can develop a parsimonious theory of effective frequency over a number of related measures.

Consumer response to a repetition of a brand's advertising differs substantially depending on consumers' prior familiarity with the brand.[31] The difference in response to brand familiarity may be due to a number of causes. First, because consumers attend to ads selectively, ads of the familiar brand may receive greater attention at lower repetitions than those of the unfamiliar brand.[32] Second, consumers may also identify with ads of the familiar brand better, because of their experience with the brand.[33] Third, to maintain consistency with their actions and beliefs, consumers may interpret ads for the familiar brands more favorably. Fourth, consumers may tire more easily with exposures to the familiar brand than they might to those of the less familiar brand. Thus, peak response may occur sooner for the familiar than for the unfamiliar brand (see Exhibit 8.6).

This issue of familiarity may be one reason for the apparent difference in results between the earlier field studies on advertising wearin and wearout, and the recent findings of John Philip Jones and Lawrence Gibson.[34] The earlier studies often experimented with fictitious messages or brands, to which respondents had no prior exposure. In such a context, advertising can keep receiving a positive response even with considerable repetition. In contrast, the latter studies focused on existing brands in mature competitive product categories. In these cases, the heavy advertisers often tend to be brands with moderate to large market share. These brands are familiar to consumers; as such their advertising needs little repetition. The study by Tellis (1988) reviewed in Chapter 6 supports this role of familiarity.[35]

Message Novelty

A second factor that is critical to the effectiveness of advertising is the novelty of the message. Some ad campaigns have become legendary because of their sustained use (and apparent effectiveness) without changes over decades. But those are examples of a few campaigns. In most cases, advertisers change their ad campaigns, either because the ad was ineffective to begin with or because the campaign has worn out. If campaigns do indeed wear out, then

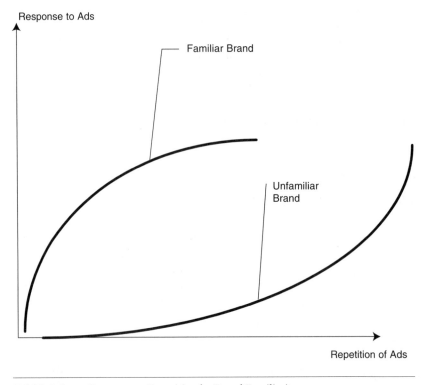

Exhibit 8.6   Response to Repetition by Brand Familiarity

would they not also wear in? The majority of studies that have examined this issue conclude that while wearout does indeed occur, wearin may not occur.[36] That is, good ad campaigns may be effective right from the first exposure, even though their effectiveness wears out after a period of time such as a couple of months to a quarter year. Recently, some major field studies have underscored this conclusion by finding positive effects for changes of a creative in an ad campaign.[37] For example, several studies found that changes in creative were more likely to have an impact on sales than dramatic increases or decreases in advertising weight (or frequency) (see Chapter 8).

An important occasion for the use of novelty is in an ad campaign that uses multiple creative executions. Examples are the campaigns for FedEx and Altoids discussed in Chapter 2. Each creative has a new drama, endorser, image, or copy to retain interest, while the common tagline links the creative executions in the campaign and reiterates the message.

Within the duration of time when a campaign is in effect, studies find that spacing out of ads as in *pulsing* (advertising at fixed intervals) or *flighting* (advertising at irregular intervals) is likely to be more effective than massing, especially if the goal of the campaign is learning of a new message.[38] A good example is Zielske's classic study (see Exhibit 8.5). This effect can also be explained by the habituation-tedium theory. Rapid repetition in a short period of time leads to tedium, lower interest, and lower attention without much increase in habituation. The result is less effectiveness of message repetition. However, delay between exposures reduces the tedium while increasing the habituation. The result is higher effectiveness of message repetition.

The two points of view differ in the way they address this issue of the novelty of the message. Repetitionists focus on the novelty of the message over the life of the campaign. Minimalists focus on the short-term effectiveness of an ad exposure independently of the campaign to which it belongs. Actually, both Jones and Gibson found some ads to be ineffective or even to have negative effects on sales.[39] Are these the ads that have worn out or run past their optimum period of effectiveness?

Message Complexity

A third important factor that moderates effective frequency is the complexity of the ad's message. A complex message is one that is sufficiently difficult, rich, or ambiguous that the receiver cannot absorb all the information it contains in a single exposure. A long line of research suggests that repetition enhances the persuasive effect of ads containing complex messages.[40] The reasons is that each repetition of an ad with a complex message allows the receiver to gain new insights about the message. This stimulation maintains the receiver's interest in the ad and delays the onset of tedium. Complex messages can take several forms including soft sell and emotional appeals (see Chapter 10).

Implications

An important implication of the role of familiarity is that brands with a large market share enjoy a double advantage. They have a larger following of consumers, who are more familiar with them, than brands that are new or have a small market share. So large-share brands need less advertising than small-share brands.[41] One solution for new or small-share brands is to induce a brand trial as a means to increase familiarity among consumers who are unaware of the brand. Such a trial can be initiated by samples, price discounts, or other promotions. The advertising of these brands may be more effective once consumers have some familiarity with them.

An important implication of the role of message complexity is the potential of soft sell and emotional appeals. Indeed, emotional appeals may be effective not only in selective products such as perfumes or sports cars but also for so-called thinking products such as cameras, insurance, or education.

A practical issue in repetition is the appropriate time period for analysis. Should the period of analysis be based on some absolute measure, the frequency of the advertising, or the purchase cycle?

The argument for an absolute measure of time is that consumer memory for ads lasts for some fixed period. But is that period an hour, day, week, or month? For example, a direct marketer that advertises on TV and offers an 800 phone number for purchases may be interested in effective frequency per hour. If response to its ad is not immediate, the pressure of competing messages and activities may dilute the impact of that ad. At the other extreme, a corporate advertiser may be interested in long-term improvements in consumer goodwill, rather than any immediate changes in behavior. In either case, the optimal level of repetition would vary by the type of change desired by the ad campaign.

The argument for adopting the purchase cycle is that each purchase so dominates a consumer's thinking that all previous advertising would have small cumulative effects. Advertising after the purchase would have the most important influence for the next purchase. The purchase cycle of a kitchen appliance is about 10 years, that of a car about 8 years, and that of a computer about 3 years, while that of a tube of toothpaste is about 4 months. In that case, optimal repetition would vary dramatically by product category.

The argument for adopting the frequency of advertising is that advertising is the cause and as such drives whatever effects one observes. Thus, in addition to the three factors described above, the practical issue of period of analysis must also be considered when determining the optimal level of repetition.

THEORIES EXPLAINING REPETITION

Researchers have put forth several theories to explain the mechanism by which repetition works. Two of these theories may be particularly relevant to advertising: habituation-tedium and conditioning.[42]

Habituation-Tedium Theory

According to this theory, a combination of two factors, habituation and tedium, mediate ad response. When subjects first see novel stimuli, the novelty leads to uncertainty and tension. Repeated exposure reduces this uncertainty and tension, leading to familiarity and liking. This process is called habituation. At the same time, the repetitive exposure to the same stimuli leads to growing boredom and decreased liking. This process is called tedium. Habituation is strong early on, while tedium is strong later on in the sequence of repetitions. The two factors together lead to an inverted-U-shaped response to repetition (see Exhibit 8.7).

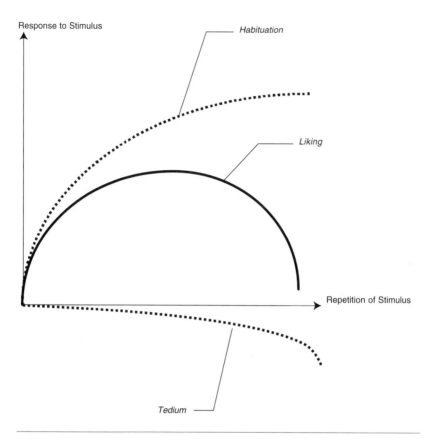

Exhibit 8.7   Repetition Persuades Through Habituation and Tedium

The habituation-tedium theory is important because it suggests that response to ad repetition is neither instantaneous nor perpetual. Rather, there is some level of repetition that may be optimum. Furthermore, based on the factor discussed above, this level could vary by brand, message, or audience characteristics. Managers would need research to identify what level of repetition is ideal in specific contexts.

Theory of Conditioning

Classical ideas about conditioning arose from the experiments of Russian physiologist Ivan Pavlov. He found that repetitive ringing of a bell before serving dogs food led them to salivate merely with the ringing of the bell, even without food. The association of the bell with food conditioned the dogs to salivate with the bell alone. Thus in principle, a conditioned response (e.g., salivation) takes

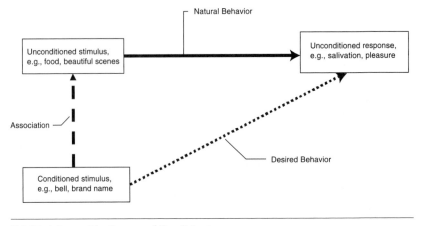

Exhibit 8.8   The Process of Conditioning

place through repetitive associations between a pair of stimuli, the unconditioned (e.g., food) and the conditioned (e.g., bell). Exhibit 8.8 presents a schematic diagram of the classical conditioning process. Once learned, a conditioned response does not require repetitive associations of the two stimuli to sustain. However, if either of the two stimuli occurs alone, then the association between the two gets weakened and leads to the ultimate loss of conditioning.

Does classical conditioning occur in humans? Can it be used in advertising? Some controlled laboratory studies do support the effectiveness of conditioning in a marketing context.[43] One study showed that repeatedly exposing subjects to an ad for a new brand of toothpaste with attractive water scenes led them to like that brand more than subjects in a control group who saw the ad without the water scenes.[44] This behavioral change is ultimately what many advertisers hope to achieve by associating their brands with attractive pictures and personalities.

Another study argued that conditioning was the primary reason for the use of happy scenes or celebrities.[45] The meaning that celebrities acquire in their careers and lives transfers onto brands when the two are repeatedly associated. In this case, the celebrity is the unconditioned stimulus, the brand is the conditioned stimulus, and the feeling of attraction is the response.

Extensive experiments have shown that four factors favor the success of conditioning: the predictiveness, distinctiveness, response strength, and link of the unconditioned stimulus.

First, the conditioned stimulus should be closely associated with the unconditioned one.[46] Second, the unconditioned stimulus should be distinct or unique. Third, the unconditioned stimulus should have a strong appeal for the recipient. Fourth, there should be a good link between the two stimuli. Conditioning may explain why repetitive association of a stimulus and a brand in advertising seems to work.

Summary

Various appeals can be classified under four heads: argument, endorsement, emotion, and passive processing. Researchers sometime group the latter three under the rubric of peripheral routes of persuasion. As discussed in the previous chapter, this classification is convenient and adequate though by no means absolute. In particular, emotion and endorsement are forms of persuasion that can take place with other forms and with each other. Rather than relying exclusively on any simple dichotomy, the following three chapters discuss the strengths, limitations, and uses of these forms of persuasion: argument, emotion, and endorsement.

How many exposures are enough? Advertisers need a simple, numerical answer to the question when scheduling an ad campaign, or deciding how often to run each ad. As stated above, the field is bifurcated with two points of view: minimalists who believe in only one or two exposures and repetitionists who believe in repeated exposures. However, as the above discussion indicates, there may be no simple, numerical answer to that question. The reason is that the effectiveness of repetition depends on many factors that change substantially from ad to ad. Three factors proposed here may be particularly important: brand familiarity, message novelty, and message complexity.

Notes

1.   For a forceful exposition of the importance of templates for creativity, see Goldenberg, Jacob, David Mazursky, and Sorin Solomon (1999), "Creativity Templates: Towards Identifying the Fundamental Schemes of Quality Advertisements," *Marketing Science*, 8, 3, 331-351.

2.   Meyers-Levy, Joan, and Prashant Malaviya (1999), "Consumers' Processing of Persuasive Advertisements: An Integrative Framework of Persuasion Theories," *Journal of Marketing* Special Issue: Fundamental issues and directions for marketing, 63, 45-60.

3.   Petty, Richard E., and John T. Cacioppo (1986), *Communication and Persuasion,* New York: Springer-Verlag. See also MacInnis, Deborah, and Bernard J. Jaworski (1990), "Two Routes to Persuasion Models in Advertising: Review, Critique, and Research Direction," *Review of Marketing*, 4, 3-42; Cacioppo, John T., and Richard E. Petty (1985), "Central and Peripheral Routes to Persuasion: The Role of Message Repetition," in Linda F. Alwitt and Andrew A. Mitchell (eds.), *Psychological Processes and Advertising Effects: Theory, Research and Applications,* Hillsdale, NJ: Lawrence Erlbaum, 90-111.

4.   Petty and Cacioppo, *Communication and Persuasion.*

5. Petty, Richard E., John T. Cacioppo, and David Schumann (1983), "Central and Peripheral Routes to Advertising Effectiveness: The Moderating Role of Involvement," *Journal of Consumer Research*, 10 (September), 135-146.

6. Sengupta, Jaideep, Ronald C. Goodstein, and David S. Boninger (1997), "All Cues Are Not Created Equal: Obtaining Attitude Persistence Under Low-Involvement Conditions," *Journal of Consumer Research*, 23, 4 (March), 351-361.

7. Petty, Richard E., Rao H. Unnava, and Alan J. Strathman (1991), "Theories of Attitude Change," in *Handbook of Consumer Behavior*, Thomas S. Robertson and Harold H. Kassarjian (eds.), Englewood Cliffs, NJ: Prentice Hall; McGuire, W. J. (1964), "Inducing Resistance to Persuasion: Some Contemporary Approaches," in *Advances in Experimental Social Psychology*, vol. 1. New York: Academic Press.

8. Schumann, David W., Richard E. Petty, and D. Scott Clemons (1990), "Predicting the Effectiveness of Different Strategies of Advertising Variation: A Test of the Repetition-Variation Hypotheses," *Journal of Consumer Research*, 17 (September), 192-202; Krugman, Herbert (1972), "Why Three Exposures May Be Enough," *Journal of Advertising Research* (February), 21-25.

9. Hawkins, Scott A., Stephen J. Hoch, and Joan Meyers-Levy (2001), "Low-Involvement Learning: Repetition and Coherence in Familiarity and Belief," *Journal of Consumer Psychology*, 11, 1 (July), 1-11; Heath, Robert (1999), "Just Popping Down to the Shops for a Packet of Image Statements: A New Theory of How Consumers Perceive Brands," *Journal of the Market Research Society*, l 41, 2 (April), 153-169; Muehling, Darrel D, Russell N. Laczniak, and J. Craig Andrews (1993), "Defining, Operationalizing and Using Involvement in Advertising Research: A Review," *Journal of Current Issues and Research in Advertising*, 15, 1 (Spring), 21-57; Celsi, Richard L., and Jerry C. Olson (1988), "The Role of Involvement in Attention and Comprehension Processes," *Journal of Consumer Research*, September 15, 210-224.

10. Kover, Arthur J. (1995), "Copywriters' Implicit Theories of Communication: An Exploration," *Journal of Consumer Research*, 21, 4 (March), 596-611.

11. Hawkins, Scott A. and Steve J. Hoch (1992), "Low-Involvement Learning: Memory Without Evaluation," *Journal of Consumer Research*, 19 (September), 212-225.

12. Examples and ideas of this section have been inspired by Sawyer, Alan (1981), "Repetition, Cognitive Responses and Persuasion," in *Cognitive Responses in Persuasion*, Richard E. Petty, Thomas M. Ostrom, and Timothy C. Brock (eds.), Hillsdale, NJ: Lawrence Erlbaum.

13. Sawyer, "Repetition, Cognitive Responses and Persuasion."

14. Schmitt, B. H. (1994), "Contextual Priming of Nonverbal Material in Advertising," *Psychology and Marketing*, 11, 1-14; Erdley, C. A., and P. R. D'Agostino (1988), "Cognitive and Affective Components of Automatic Priming Effects," *Journal of Personality and Social Psychology*, 54, 741-747.

15. Ha, Young-Won, and Stephen J. Hoch (1989), "Ambiguity, Processing, and Advertising-Evidence Interactions," *Journal of Consumer Research*, 16 (December), 354-360; Braun, Kathryn A. (1999), "Postexperience Advertising Effects on Consumer Memory," *Journal of Consumer Research*, 25, 4 (March), 319-334.

16. Wright, Alice A., and John G. Lynch, Jr. (1995), "Communication Effects of Advertising Versus Direct Experience When Both Search and Experience Attributes Are Present," *Journal of Consumer Research*, 21, 4 (March), 708-718.

17. Packard, Vance (1957), *Hidden Persuaders*, New York: Simon & Schuster.

18. Synodinos, Nicolaos (1988), "Subliminal Stimulation: What Does the Public Think About It?" *Current Research and Issues in Advertising*, 11, 1, 157-187.

19. Trappey, Charles (1996), "A Meta-Analysis of Consumer Choice and Subliminal Advertising," *Psychology and Marketing*, 13, 5 (August), 517-530.

20. Rogers, Stuart (1994), "Subliminal Advertising: Grand Scam of the 20th Century," in *Proceedings of the 1994 Conference of the Academy of Advertising*, Karen Whitehall King (ed.), Athens, GA: American Academy of Advertising.

21. Rogers, "Subliminal Advertising,"

22. Synodinos, "Subliminal Stimulation."

23. Krugman, "Why Three Exposures."

24. McDonald, Colin (1971), "What Is the Short-Term Effect of Advertising?" Marketing Science Institute Report No. 71-142, Cambridge, MA: Marketing Science Institute.

25. Naples, Michael J. (1979), *Effective Frequency: The Relationship Between Frequency and Advertising Effectiveness*, New York: Association of National Advertisers.

26. Jones, John Philip (1990), "Ad Spending: Maintaining Market Share," *Harvard Business Review*, 38-41; Gibson, Lawrence D. (1996), "What Can One TV Exposure Do," *Journal of Advertising Research* (March/April), 9-18.

27. Zielske, Hubert A. (1959), "The Remembering and Forgetting of Advertising," *Journal of Marketing*, 23, 1, 239-243.

28. Sawyer, "Repetition, Cognitive Responses and Persuasion."

29. Craig, C. Samuel, Brian Sternthal, and Clark Leavitt (1976), "Advertising Wearout: An Experimental Analysis," *Journal of Marketing Research*, 13 (November), 356-372.

30. Sawyer, "Repetition, Cognitive Responses and Persuasion"; Tellis, Gerard J. (1988), "Advertising Exposure, Loyalty and Brand Purchase: A Two Stage Model of Choice," *Journal of Marketing Research*, 25 (May), 134-144.

31. Tellis, "Advertising Exposure, Loyalty and Brand Purchase"; Mehta, Abhilasha (2000), "Advertising Attitudes and Advertising Effectiveness," *Journal of Advertising Research*, 40, 3 (May-June), 67-72.

32. Sawyer, "Repetition, Cognitive Responses and Persuasion."

33. Hoch, Stephen J., and John Deighton (1989), "Managing What Consumers Learn From Experience," *Journal of Marketing*, 53 (April), 1-20.

34. Jones, "Ad Spending"; Gibson, "What Can One TV Exposure Do."

35. Tellis, "Advertising Exposure, Loyalty and Brand Purchase."

36. Pechmann, Cornelia, and David W. Stewart, (1992) "Advertising Repetition: A Critical Review of Wearin and Wearout," *Current Issues and Research in Advertising*, 11, 2, 285-330.

37. Tellis, Gerard J., Rajesh Chandy, and Pattana Thaivanich (2000), "Decomposing the Effects of Direct Advertising: Which Brand Works, When, Where, and How Long?" *Journal of Marketing Research*, 37 (February), 32-46; Eastlack, Joseph O., Jr., and Ambar G. Rao (1989), "Advertising Experiments at the Campbell Soup Company," *Marketing Science*, 8 (Winter), 57-71; Batra, Rajeev, et al. (1995), "When Does Advertising Have an Impact? A Study of Tracking Data," *Journal of Advertising Research* (September/October), 19.

38. Mahajan, Vijay, and Eitan Muller (1986), "Advertising Pulsing Policies for Generating Awareness for New Products," *Marketing Science*, 5, 2 (Spring), 89-106. Also see subsequent comments.

39. Jones, "Ad Spending"; Gibson, "What Can One TV Exposure Do."

40. Sawyer, "Repetition, Cognitive Responses and Persuasion"; Pechmann and Stewart, "Advertising Repetition."

41. Jones, "Ad Spending"; Tellis, "Advertising Exposure, Loyalty and Brand Purchase."

42. A third theory is that advertising serves as a signal of quality. High level of advertising suggests a product is of high quality but excessive advertising may trigger consumers' suspicions about quality. Such assumptions by consumers would also lead to an inverted-U-shaped response to advertising. See Kirmani, Amna (1997), "Advertising Repetition as a Signal of Quality: If It's Advertised So Much, Something Must Be Wrong," *Journal of Advertising*, 26, 3 (Fall), 77-86.

43.   Shimp, Terrence A. (1991),"Neo-Pavlovian Conditioning and Its Implications for Consumer Theory and Research," in *Handbook of Consumer Behavior,* Thomas S. Robertson and Harold H. Kassarjian (eds.), Englewood Cliffs, NJ: Prentice Hall, 162-187.

44.   Stuart, Elnora W., Terrence A. Shimp, and Randall W. Engle (1987), "Classical Conditioning of Consumer Attitudes: Four Experiments in an Advertising Context," *Journal of Consumer Research,* 14 (December), 334-349.

45.   McCracken, Grant (1989), "Who Is the Celebrity Endorser? Cultural Foundations of the Endorsement Process," *Journal of Consumer Research,* 16 (December), 310-321.

46.   McSweeney, Frances K., and Calvin Bierley (1984), "Recent Developments in Classical Conditioning," *Journal of Consumer Research,* 11 (September), 619-631; Janiszewski, Chris, and Luk Warlop (1993), "The Influence of Classical Conditioning Procedures on Subsequent Attention to the Conditioned Brand," *Journal of Consumer Research,* 20 (September), 171-189.

9

Argument in Advertising

How Argument Persuades

Argument involves the central route of persuasion. It persuades a viewer of a message by appealing to reason and relying on evidence. Argument proceeds on the assumption that there is objective evidence. Viewers, especially if they have opinions or preferences contrary to the message, are likely to respond with counterarguments.[1] The effort required of viewers to think through the message and the message's stimulation of counterarguments are the major problems with the use of logic.

Persuasion via this implies that receivers of a message typically carry out the following activities:[2]

- Attend to the message and the evidence in the ad.
- Recall relevant information from their memory.
- Generate counterarguments, if any, based on that information.
- Evaluate the merits of the proposed arguments against their counterarguments.
- Draw conclusions about the issues at hand.
- Arrive at an overall opinion, attitude change, or decision to act.

If the process leads to a predominance of favorable thoughts about the message, the message is accepted. The ad persuades the consumer. A predominance of negative thoughts leads to a rejection of the message. If negative and positive thoughts are about equal, or if neutral thoughts dominate, consumers do not change their opinion, attitude, or behavior. In the latter two situations, the ad fails to persuade the consumer. Thus, the strength of the evidence relative to what the consumer recalls from memory and the strength of the argument relative to the consumer's counterarguments are the key to persuasion.

Counterarguments occur more when a message is inconsistent with a receiver's prevailing preferences.[3] Thus, persuasion is more difficult in such a context.

Besides the effort required of viewers and the stimulation of counterarguments, the use of argument also runs another major risk: miscommunication by the recipient of the message.

Argument Strategy

Advertisers can use many strategies to persuade consumers with argument and information. At least six of them are important enough to merit discussion: comparative, refutational, rhetorical, innoculative, framing, and supportive arguments.[4] The theory and evidence in support of each of these strategies are presented below.

COMPARATIVE ARGUMENT

The term *comparative argument* refers to a message that compares the target brand to some competitive standard. One of three types of standards may be used: a named competing brand, an unnamed competing brand, or a general industry standard.[5]

Before 1970, comparative ads were rare, being discouraged by the Federal Trade Commission (FTC), and avoided by skeptical firms and agencies. Several reasons motivated this behavior. Regulators probably believed that comparative advertising confused or misled consumers or that large firms would take undue advantage of small firms. Advertisers and their agencies feared that such advertising would create legal problems for the advertised brands while giving free exposure for the rival brand used in the comparison. In addition, they feared that comparative ads could lead to negative claims and advertising.

However, under pressure from consumer advocates, the FTC changed its policy in 1971 and began actively encouraging firms to use comparative advertising. The new thinking was motivated by a belief that specific information about brands, especially of the comparative kind, would help consumers make more informed decisions. Moreover, to the extent such information was truthful and substantiated, it could help superior brands to advertise that fact, improving consumer choices and increasing market efficiency. In addition, comparative claims, even when negatively framed, can still help the advertised brands under certain conditions.[6]

Since that time, comparative advertising has increased steadily as the following estimates by different authors in different years suggest:[7]

Proportion of Ads Using Comparative Advertising

Year	Proportion
1973	7%
1977	5% to 10%
1980	14%
1982	23%
1984	35%
1986	50% of NBC TV spots

A study of magazine advertisements in the United States showed that the proportion of comparative ads stayed fairly constant at about 22% between 1980 and 1990.[8] These figures, and also those of other surveys, indicate that advertisers and their agencies seem to have enough faith in comparative advertising that it has come to be a substantial part of advertising.[9] They believe that comparative advertising helps establish a brand position, initiate trial, and gain credibility. These benefits are plausible because a comparison of a target brand with certain known brands would clarify its competitive position, and if the target brand is a new brand it could lead to more credibility in its claim and its trial.

On the other hand, practitioners believe that comparative advertising is not effective in creating positive feelings, positive attitudes, or loyalty to the advertised brand. Here again the reason might be that the comparative ad, which tends to be critical of a rival, has a note of negativism about it and may offend ardent supporters of the rival brand.

An extensive review of the literature suggests that comparative ads are more effective than noncomparative ads in generating attention, message awareness, brand awareness, message processing, and purchasing intentions.[10] However, comparative ads are not *universally* more effective than noncomparative ads. Rather, two conditions favor the effectiveness of comparative ads over noncomparative ones: two-sided appeals and inferior competitive position.

Two-Sided Appeals

Message sidedness refers to whether a message contains a one-sided or a two-sided appeal. A *one-sided* appeal involves all positive statements of the advertised brand, or negative statements of the rival brand if included. A *two-sided* appeal contains some pros and cons of the advertised brand and the rival brand if included. A two-sided appeal is likely to be more effective because it overcomes two problems with persuasive appeals especially in comparative advertising.

First, no brand is likely to have all pros or be entirely free from defects; similarly, no rival brand is likely to be entirely flawed. A two-sided appeal is more credible because it suggests that the communicator is sufficiently removed from the advertised brand as to acknowledge some of its cons, or some of the pros of the rival.

Second, comparative advertising tends to motivate counterarguing by the audience.[11] Two-sided appeals have the potential to reduce such counterarguing by acknowledging and then addressing some of these arguments.[12] Indeed, a well-designed two-sided ad will directly address such counterarguments: It should start by acknowledging a brand's weaknesses (or a rival's strength), but then emphasize the brand's strengths (or the rival's weaknesses). This is especially true if the rival is the pioneer, the market-share leader, or a strongly liked brand. For example, an ad that says, "We cost more but are worth it" acknowledges a brand's high price but makes a virtue of it.

One study provides direct support for the effectiveness of comparative two-sided appeals, as shown in Exhibit 9.1.[13] Note from the exhibit that a comparative claim is inferior to a noncomparative claim in winning acceptance when a one-sided appeal is used. However, with a two-sided appeal, the comparative is much better. So, if advertisers plan to use a comparative ad, a two-sided appeal would be much better. Notice also that of the four combinations, a two-sided comparative is the best, while a one-sided comparative is the worst.

A review of research on two-sided ads suggests the following conclusions:[14]

- Two-sided appeals are more interesting and credible.
- Credibility gains are at an optimum for a moderate amount of negative information. Too little or too much negative information hurts the advocated position.
- The negative information should occur early on in the ad but not at the beginning.
- Two-sided appeals work best when the audience's position is unfavorable to the one being advocated.

Competitive Position

Competitive position is the place of a brand relative to the rival named in the comparative ad. We can identify three important aspects of the rival: share of market (small or large), order of entry (early or new), and loyalty (strong or weak). A *dominant* brand is one that has a large share, has an early entrant, or has strong loyalty, and a *small* brand is one that has the opposite qualifications. In which of these paired conditions should a brand compare itself to its rival? The answer is fairly intuitive: when the brand is small rather than dominant. For example, in election campaigns, front-runners rarely, if ever, run ads comparing themselves to the other candidates. However, less well-known candidates routinely run aggressive ads, comparing themselves to the front-runner. Why so? At least three reasons account for this position.

First, comparative advertising leads consumers to view the two compared brands as similar.[15] Such an effect is better for a small-share, new, or less-liked

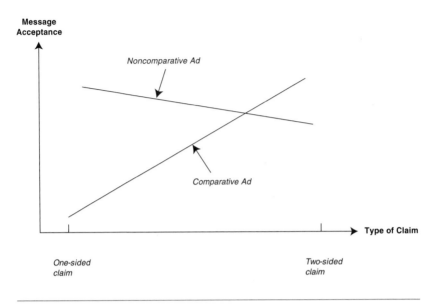

Exhibit 9.1   Message Sidedness Versus Comparison in Ad Effectiveness

SOURCE: Adapted from Swinyard, William, R. (1981), "The Interaction Between Comparative Advertising and Copy Claims Variation," *Journal of Marketing Research*, 18 (May), 175-186.

brand. Second, comparative advertising gives a rival brand free exposure. A dominant brand that is already well known to a population is unlikely to benefit much from this free exposure, especially if it is associated with mention of its negatives. However, a small brand can benefit from exposure especially if it involves comparisons with the leader, even if that involves some negatives. Third, comparative advertising prompts counterarguing by consumers, increases their dislike for both brands, and leads to an ad war. For any of these effects, a dominant brand has more to suffer than a small one.

REFUTATIONAL ARGUMENT

The strategy of *refutational advertising* consists of first presenting a counterargument against the advertised brand, and then destroying that argument. Thus, refutation is a special form of a two-sided argument. A refutational ad can be used for three purposes. First, it can be used to refute a widely held negative belief. An example would be the city of New York targeting an ad to teenagers that refutes the idea that illegal drugs are cool. Second, it can be used to refute negative implications about a brand stemming from some recent event. Third, it can be used to refute a belief or claim about a rival.

For example, Mercedes-Benz probably has the reputation for having the highest resale value among luxury cars. However, at one time, data from the National Automobile Dealers Association's (NADA) Official Used Car Guide showed that BMW had the highest resale value in this category. BMW ran a print ad with these data and the headline "Information That Mercedes-Benz Would Rather Keep Classified."

Another example is the ad campaign that popularized the Volkswagen Beetle. The brand did not do well when it was first introduced in the United States in the 1950s because consumers preferred large, sleek cars to the small, ugly Beetle. The agency handling the account (Doyle, Dane, Bernbach) proceeded to make a virtue of its weakness. In provocative ads beginning in 1959, including one called "Think Small," the firm directly attacked the preconceptions of the audience and emphasized the uniqueness of the Beetle. As a result, the small, ugly Beetle was able to carve a strong niche for itself. That loyalty was so strong that 30 years later when Volkswagen launched a new model on the old design, Beetle loyalists snapped it up at a premium price.

Is refutational advertising effective? Why and when?

Why Refutational Argument Is Effective

Research indicates that refutational advertising is effective because it directly addresses the concerns of the audience. As stated before, persuasive messages tend to trigger some counterarguing on the part of the message recipient. This counterarguing is more severe if it involves some widely held negative belief about the advertised brand that is neither addressed nor mentioned in the ad. In such circumstance, braving the facts and bringing up the negatives and then destroying them are both more satisfying to the audience and probably more effective. Of course, for this strategy to be effective, the brand must have some new, unambiguous information that can refute its existing negatives. Also, if the refutation involves comparative advertising, these facts should not be so narrow that a rival brand itself can easily refute them, leading to an ad war that renders both brands in a poorer light. For example, at one time, refutational ads between anti-ulcer drugs Tagamet and Pepcid became so intense, with so many claims and counterclaims, that a judge had to order both advertisers to refrain from comparative or refutational advertising until he could sort out the issues.[16]

When Refutational Argument Is Effective

The prior example suggests that refutational advertising is not a strategy to be used indiscriminately but one that may be effective given certain conditions. These conditions are defined by the presence of widely held and enduring negative beliefs about the brand and no ambiguity about the issues involved.

Widely held negative belief. Most important, the claim or belief to be refuted must be held by a large proportion of the population. For example, Honda's and Toyota's superiority over Nissan may have been widely believed, so an ad emphasizing the contrary with new information would be interesting and relevant.

Enduring negative belief. The claim or belief that is to be refuted must be of an enduring nature, not temporary. Often during a crisis, a firm or brand gets a great deal of negative publicity. However, if the crisis is carefully handled through public relations, with apologies for wrongdoing, promises of remedial work, or strong defenses of the firm's integrity, then the press is likely to let off and the crisis likely to subside. A refutational campaign not only may be unnecessary but may reinforce the negatives. For example, in the mid-1990s, reports surfaced of needles and syringes in Pepsi and Diet Pepsi cans. Pepsi responded through its public relations department with strong defenses of its manufacturing integrity. At the same time, the company ran a massive TV ad campaign using supportive appeals with no mention of the crisis. The reports were found to be false, and the crisis passed.[17] In contrast, the belief of Honda's and Toyota's superiority over Nissan was probably enduring so that a refutational ad by Nissan was justified.

Unambiguous issues. The issues surrounding the claims and counterclaims of the refutational ad should be unambiguous. There was no ambiguity when BMW topped the resale value tables. Thus, a campaign refuting consumers' long-standing perception that BMW is inferior to Mercedes-Benz would have been in order.

Attack by Rival

A rebuttal ad is one that seeks to immediately refute a comparative ad of a rival in which the current brand is attacked or criticized. Research indicates that failure to rebut a rival's attack leads to belief in the rival's criticism of the current brand.[18]

Refutational arguments run the risk of providing exposure to rival positions. Also, refutational arguments tend to contain negatives as the ad tries to tear down the rival's position. Both of these situations can lead to misunderstandings especially as audiences are busy and not always fully attuned to the message in an ad. Misunderstandings are especially prevalent when using negatives or double negatives. Thus, when writing copy for such arguments, as also for all other copy writing, advertisers need to follow the same elementary principles of good writing used by journalists and novelists who face a busy or uninterested audience.

- Write simply with the reader in mind.
- Use small, simple words.
- Use short, simple sentences.
- Use concrete rather than abstract words.
- Draw conclusions rather than leave the audience with suggestions.
- Minimize negatives and avoid double negatives.

RHETORICAL QUESTION

A subtle way of attacking a rival's position is to ask a question rather than make a counterattack. For example, consider Target planning an ad against a rival, Wal-Mart. Wal-Mart's ads typically have a tagline that says, "Always low prices." Target could run an ad that asks, "Are Wal-Mart's prices always the lowest?" This approach to arguments has many advantages.

First, it contains no arguments; thus, it does not provoke any counterarguments among viewers. Second, it plants a seed against the rival that can grow into an argument. Third, it associates the rival with a negative thought or premise, albeit weakly so. Fourth, it gets the receiver of the message to do the thinking or research to answer that question. As a result, message recipients generate thoughts that are likely to relate to the rival position. In this case, the thoughts might revolve around why Wal-Mart might not have the lowest prices. Irrespective of the validity of those thoughts, they still represent arguments against the rival brand (Wal-Mart). Fifth, should the message recipient encounter any claim or evidence in favor of the rival brand, this question will cast some doubt over it.

Rhetorical questions might be most effective when the rival is liked without enough justification or the issues are sensitive. By asking probing questions, the advertiser can sow doubt about the rival without appearing to attack it. As such, the advertisers can avoid antagonizing the message recipient or putting him or her on the defensive. Research shows that merely asking questions of respondents leads them to behavior about which the question was asked.[19] The probable reasons may be a priming effect, discussed in Chapter 8.[20] Rhetorical questions are not common in advertising. Thus, they represent a highly promising route of argument and persuasion.

INNOCULATIVE ARGUMENT

An innoculative ad is one that protects a brand's position with current consumers by alerting them about and helping them to defend against an impending attack. Is innoculative advertising possible? Why? In medicine, inoculating individuals involves infecting them with a weakened dose of the disease that their immune system can easily withstand. The immune system is then sensitized and can deal effectively with the more virulent form of the real disease if it comes along.

A similar principle applies in this strategy. We saw in the material above that consumers' attention and perception are selective, which leads them to resist change and hold on to their current beliefs and practices. However, when faced with strong arguments to change to a rival brand, they may accept the new position if they are motivated and able to process the new information. Innoculative advertising presents the rival's position with weak forms of the arguments, followed by strong counterarguments that refute the position.

Some evidence does support innoculative advertising.[21] In general, defensive marketing (i.e., giving a consumer good arguments to withstand an attack by a rival) is more effective and less costly than offensive marketing (i.e., trying to win consumers back after they have switched to the rival's point of view). The main reason may be that consumers generate more counterarguments against messages that are inconsistent with their prevailing preferences than against those consistent with their prevailing preferences.[22] Thus, it is easier to persuade a neutral or favorable consumer than one who is already convinced of the competition's claim.

Support for innoculative arguments also comes from research on primacy versus recency effects. A review of these studies indicates that when consumers are involved in issues, they are more responsive to the first position (primary) to which they have been exposed than to a later position (recency effect). However, when they are not involved in the issues, they are more responsive to the recent position to which they have been exposed than to the first one.[23] The reason for the difference is that involvement leads to greater elaboration on the issues and thus greater understanding, persuasion, and recall, which seem to favor the position consumers encountered first.

Innoculative advertising can be an effective means to defend against new brand entry, price drops by rivals, or major promotional events of rivals. This strategy is especially useful if the defending firm cannot and does not think it prudent to match the rivals' specific efforts in products, features, or price.

FRAMING

Framing is the presentation of a rival in a context that makes it less attractive. Framing is powerful because it does not involve explicit criticisms of the rival, which might raise the defenses or arouse the sympathy of viewers. Rather, it involves introduction of subtle pieces of information that change the reference point of viewers.

One form of framing is to advertise contrary claims of a rival. Another is to advertise contradictions between claims and reality of a rival. A third is to mildly exaggerate the claims of a rival until they appear incredible. Hyperbole and sarcasm are forms of framing.

Framing is effective when the target segment does not have all the information about a rival. When effectively used, it can be a subtle means of making a damning statement about a rival. Although the word *framed* is sometimes used casually to mean someone was wrongly accused, here it does not necessarily imply deception or impropriety.

SUPPORTIVE ARGUMENT

A supportive argument involves an affirmation of the positive attributes of a brand without any comparison, refutation, inoculation, framing, or rhetorical question or statement. It is by far the simplest and most common strategy. Supportive arguments are appropriate when one needs to use evidence and appeal to reason, but there is no advantage to any of the other argument strategies discussed above.

The supportive argument is a plain-vanilla argument. However, it is not ineffective. It is particularly relevant for a leading or dominant brand that is doing well and not under duress or attack. It can also work well for a new brand establishing a new category for which consumers still do not have strong prior opinions or strong preferences.

For example, Gillette regularly introduces new brands that are superior to its older brands. In advertising for the new brand, the firm uses supportive arguments that clearly emphasize the features of the new brand. It avoids comparative arguments with prevailing brands, because it already owns the leading brands and wants to avoid cannibalizing sales of its own brands.

Summary

Arguments involve the central route of persuasion. They tend to trigger counterarguments on the part of the recipient. Message recipients decide by weighing the arguments and evidence for and against the advertised message. A preponderance of arguments in favor of the advertised message leads to its acceptance, while a preponderance against it leads to its rejection.

To persuade consumers, advertisers can craft information into a variety of arguments. Five characteristic types of arguments are supportive, comparative, refutational, rhetorical, innoculative, and framing. The effective use of these strategies depends on the recipient's state of mind, the position of the brand in the market, the type of information available, and the advertising context.

Notes

1.   Jain, Shailendra Pratap, and Durairaj Maheswaran (2000), "Motivated Reasoning: A Depth-of-Processing Perspective," *Journal of Consumer Research*, 26, 4 (March), 358-371.

2.   Petty, Richard E., and John T. Cacioppo (1986), *Communication and Persuasion*, New York: Springer-Verlag.

3.   Jain and Maheswaran, "Motivated Reasoning."

4.   McGuire, William J. (1964), "Inducing Resistance to Persuasion: Some Contemporary Approaches," in *Advances in Experimental Social Psychology*, vol. 1, New York: Academic Press; Aaker, David A., Rajeev Batra, and John G. Myers (1992), *Advertising Management*, Englewood Cliffs, NJ: Prentice Hall.

5.   Muehling, Darrel D., Donald E. Stem, Jr., and Peter Raven (1989), "Comparative Advertising: Views From Advertisers, Agencies, Media and Policy Makers," *Journal of Advertising Research* (October/November), 38-48.

6.   Shiv, Baba, Julie A. Edell, and John W. Payne (1997), "Factors Affecting the Impact of Negatively and Positively Framed Ad Messages," *Journal of Consumer Research*, 24, 3 (December), 285-294.

7.   Rogers, John C., and Terrell G. Williams (1989), "Comparative Advertising Effectiveness: Practitioners Perceptions Versus Academic Research Findings," *Journal of Advertising Research* (October/November), 22-37.

8.   James, Karen E., John Fraedrich, and Paul J Hensel (1995), "Comparative Magazine Advertisements Revisited: A Content Analysis," Southern Marketing Association, Orlando, FL (November 8-11), http://www.sbaer.uca.edu/Research/1995/SMA/95swa109.htm.

9.   Rogers and Williams, "Comparative Advertising Effectiveness."

10.   Grewal, Dhruv, et al. (1997), "Comparative Versus Non-comparative Advertising: A Meta-Analysis," *Journal of Marketing*, 61 (October), 1-15.

11.   Gorn, Gerald J., and Charles B. Weinberg (1984), "The Impact of Comparative Advertising on Perception and Attitude: Some Positive Findings," *Journal of Consumer Research*, 11 (September), 719-727.

12.   The Gorn and Weinberg (1984) study provides indirect support for this hypothesis by showing that respondents had less counterarguments to comparative ads when also exposed to ads of rival brands. They hypothesize that showing rivals' ads created an air of fairness. The same principle might work if the rival's position were first presented in a two-sided argument.

13.   Swinyard, William R. (1981), "The Interaction Between Comparative Advertising and Copy Claim Variation," *Journal of Marketing Research*, 18 (May), 175-186.

14.   Crowley, Ayn E., and Wayne D. Hoyer (1994), "An Integrative Framework for Understanding Two-Sided Persuasion," *Journal of Consumer Research*, 20, 4 (March), 561-575.

15.   Gorn and Weinberg, "The Impact of Comparative Advertising."

16.   Mathews, Jay (1995), "Judge Bars Firms' Competing Claims for Stomach Drugs," *Washington Post*, October 15, A2.

17.   Horovitz, Bruce (1993), "Pepsi Takes Offensive Against Image Fizz," *Los Angeles Times*, June 17, D1.

18.   Weigold, Michael F., and Vivian Sheer (1993), "Negative Political Ads: Effects of Target Response and Party-Based Expectancies on Candidate Evaluations," American Academy of Advertising, Montreal Conference Proceedings, 117.

19.   Morwitz, Vicki G., Eric Johnson, and David C. Schmittlein (1993), "Does Measuring Intent Change Behavior?" *Journal of Consumer Research*, 20 (June), 46-61.

20.   Fitzsimons, Gavan, and V. Morwitz (1996), "The Effect of Measuring Intent on Brand-Level Purchase Behavior," *Journal of Consumer Research*, 23.

21.   Bither, Stewart W., Ira J. Dolich, and Elaine B. Nell (1971), "The Application of Attitude Immunization Technique in Marketing," *Journal of Marketing Research*, 8 (February), 56-61.

22.   Jain and Maheswaran, "Motivated Reasoning."

23.   Haugtvedt, Curtis P., and Duane T. Wegener (1994), "Message Order Effects in Persuasion: An Attitude Strength Perspective," *Journal of Consumer Research*, 21, 1 (June), 205-215.

10

Emotion in Advertising

M any people assume that the most effective advertising consists of arguments supported by clear evidence. Many people also think that emotional or funny ads are frivolous and ineffective; the only ads that work are those that embody strong arguments. These beliefs rely on the assumption that most consumers make decisions based on the comparative performance of rival brands on specific characteristics. Actually, as suggested in the previous chapter, the use of emotions can be an effective and powerful means of persuasion.

Emotion is probably one of the least understood of mental activities. Indeed, until recently advertising researchers did not focus much on emotions. Over the past decade, that situation has begun to change, though our understanding of emotions is still fairly elementary.

This chapter defines *emotion* as a state of arousal. For example, anger, pride, affection, and sadness all imply certain levels and qualities of arousal. Researchers can measure this arousal as specific types and levels of biochemical activity in the body. Examples are alertness, sweating, or rapid heartbeat. Emotions are distinct from thoughts. Yet emotions are typically aroused or dissipated through a sequence of thoughts triggered by stimuli, for example, a sad story causing sadness. The association of stimuli (e.g., thunder and lightning) with certain emotions (e.g., fear) takes place through conditioning. Once the link has been established, the emotion can be triggered even without thinking, and even when rational thought suggests the emotion is unwarranted. Thus, emotions are powerful human energies that exist independently of reasoning.

Humans are capable of a vast array of emotions with many subtle variations.[1] For advertisers, the four important issues are how do emotions work, when do emotions work, how to arouse these emotions, and which particular emotions to arouse. The three subsequent sections address each of these issues.

How Do Emotions Work?

This chapter first discusses how emotion works relative to logic and then presents the advantages and disadvantages of emotion.

MODES OF PERSUASION

The arousal of emotions persuades viewers in a way that is quite different from that of argument (see Chapter 9). The communicator uses various stimuli that are likely to stimulate emotions. These stimuli may be characters, pictures, music, sequences of events, or humor. The stimuli are more interesting, easier to follow, and easier to recall than arguments. The aroused emotion then persuades the recipient to action in one of three modes: implicit, explicit, or associative.[2]

Implicit Mode

In the *implicit mode*, the advertiser arouses emotions while embedding a message in characters involved in a plot. The characters are so real and the plot so interesting that it captures the attention of the viewers and immerses them in the roles of the characters. The emotion also lowers their defenses against the message. Viewers empathize or *feel with* the characters and believe the message.[3] The persuasion in this mode is implicit: There may be no arguments and no direct attribute claims (see Exhibit 10.1A).

Explicit Mode

In the *explicit mode*, the advertiser arouses emotions using stimuli to drive home a point of view. In contrast to the implicit mode, the advertiser explicitly makes the claim and may support it with arguments (see Exhibit 10.1B). However, the persuasion occurs primarily through the arousal of emotion rather than the force of the argument. The emotions raised are of sympathy (feeling for or against events or actors) rather than of empathy as in the implicit mode.[4] An example is an antiabortion ad that graphically shows the destruction of a fetus. The ad does make an explicit argument against abortion. But it achieves its goal with stimuli that arouse great guilt and loathing for the consequences of abortion. These strong emotions can motivate a viewer to avoid the action, even if she rationally felt it justified.

Associative Mode

The *associative mode* arouses emotions with stimuli that are only tangentially related to the product (see Exhibit 10.1C). For example, a McDonald's ad shows Kobe Bryant teaching a young child to play basketball. The ad arouses a

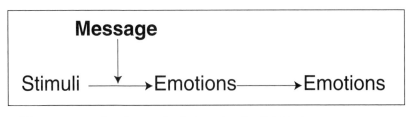

Exhibit 10.1A   Modes of Persuasion by Emotion: Implicit Mode

Exhibit 10.1B   Modes of Persuasion by Emotion: Explicit Mode

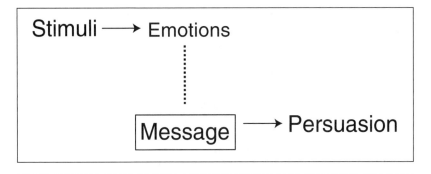

Exhibit 10.1C   Modes of Persuasion by Emotion: Associative Mode

great deal of warmth without claiming any product benefit. In this case, the drama draws the audience into the action and lets the audience share the warm feeling. The purpose of the ad is to capture the audience's attention and to associate the McDonald's name with a feeling for warmth. Thus, persuasion occurs through better recall of the brand name and its association with warmth, rather through any explicit or implicit brand attribute.

Thus, emotion can be an independent means of persuasion as in the *implicit mode*, or it can work with argument and endorsements as in the other two modes. The advantages of emotion can be best achieved when it is used alone. When combined with argument or endorsement, the advantages of emotion are not as strong, but some of its limitations are lessened. We now consider these advantages and disadvantages in detail.

ADVANTAGES OF EMOTION

Emotion has several advantages over logic. First, emotion, especially if it relies on the *implicit* or associative route, does not raise the viewers' natural defenses. The emotion-arousing stimuli draw the viewers into the action and distract them from the advertiser's intention to persuade.

Second, emotion requires less effort from the viewer. When following logic, a viewer has to carefully attend to and evaluate the argument. Pictures, music, or actions that arouse emotion require far less cognitive effort on the part of a viewer.

Third, emotion-arousing stimuli are generally more interesting. A plot, especially one that arises from conflict among characters, tends to be captivating. An argument that has a number of facts bound together by logic is not intrinsically or universally as interesting.

Fourth, emotion-arousing stimuli such as pictures and music are easier to recall than is factual evidence.[5] Moreover, emotions themselves may endure in memory far longer than arguments. For example, some Vietnam veterans still suffer from uncontrollable fear when they hear thunder during a storm. The reason is that they experienced extreme fear in an attack that occurred in the midst of a storm with thunder and lightning.

Fifth, emotion may lead to behavior change more immediately than logic would. Consider the following examples:

- People for the Ethical Treatment of Animals (PETA), an animal rights group, prepares promotional material that depicts cute animals that are subjected to ghastly experiments in Gillette's laboratories. The graphic pictures and horror stories immediately prompt children and adults to boycott Gillette's product, write to Gillette, and even threaten Gillette's employees with violence. Gillette responds with figures that show that its laboratory tests conform with all federal regulations, are declining in number, are essential for human safety, and constitute legally acceptable evidence. However, PETA's use of emotion is far more effective than Gillette's resort to reason.
- Pro-life activists argue their cause by showing graphic scenes of singing children interspersed with pictures of dead fetuses. The images arouse such strong feelings of horror and guilt among viewers as to win immediate converts to the cause of opposing abortions.
- During the 1970s, various reports and promotional material from consumer groups described stories of how Nestlé's promotions for infant formula in developing countries led to unnecessary illness and death of infants. The (debatable) conclusion from these stories that "Nestlé's kills babies" created such an outrage in the United States that it pressured Nestlé into revamping its strategy.

DISADVANTAGES OF EMOTION

Emotion also has some disadvantages relative to logic.

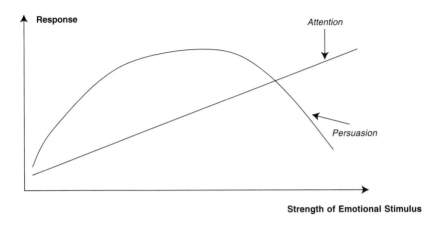

Exhibit 10.2   Attention and Persuasion in Response to Emotional Appeal

First, the arousal of emotions, especially indirectly with a story, generally requires more time than the communication of a message through argument. As a result, there is not as much space or time to communicate the product benefits in detail as when using argument.

Second, viewers could get so involved in the emotions that they may miss the central message. For example, an ad with grotesque images or brilliant colors may rivet consumers' attention to the stimulus but lead them to ignore the message. One study showed that sexy illustrations in ads were only a little better in gaining readership and immediate recall of a brand name than similar nonsexy ads.[6] However, recall after a week was much lower for ads with the sexy illustrations. Apparently, subjects may have noted the ad because of the sexiness of the illustration, but had not focused enough on the brand and message to recall it later on. Similarly, research shows that while sex appeals are effective in drawing attention, they may not help in driving home the message. In general, attention to an ad probably increases with the strength of the emotion, but persuasion reaches some maximum level and then begins to fall (see Exhibit 10.2). To avoid this dropoff in persuasion, the emotional stimulus needs to be closely linked to the message.[7]

Third, negative emotions (e.g., fear, sorrow) may be so unpleasant that viewers may just screen out the stimuli and the message. For example, ads that show extreme family suffering caused by alcoholics may prompt some alcoholics to deny it applies to them and so reject the message.

Fourth, the arousal of strong emotions may lead some or all of the audience to feel that the communicator is exploiting a situation. For example, at one time, Benetton often used highly emotive themes of love, war, disease, and social discord in ads for its clothing. One dramatic ad showed a father caring for his son, who was dying of AIDS. An AIDS service organization criticized the ad for using controversial and arresting images "to sell clothing."[8] Other ads that have similarly antagonized audiences included a bloody newborn child with an intact umbilical cord, a black woman breast-feeding a white baby, a nun kissing a priest, and pictures of U.S. convicts on death row.

What makes an ad appear to exploit people's emotions? The absence of a link between the emotion-arousing stimulus and the message is probably the cause of the appearance of exploitation. There is no apparent link between Benetton's clothes and the themes in its ad. In contrast, some Michelin ads are very appealing because the link between stimulus and message is clear and strong (see Exhibit 10.3). In general, ads that have a better link with the brand or the message are likely to be more effective.[9] Emotion that uses the implicit or explicit mode tends to have a stronger and more explicit link than that which uses the associative mode.

When Do Emotions Work?

The prior discussion suggests that neither logic nor emotion is universally superior. Each has advantages and disadvantages that indicate times when each may preferably be used. When should one use emotion rather than logic? Three factors can be used to answer this question in the context of purchase behavior: the audience's involvement in the purchase decision, the product being purchased, and the mood of the audience.

When an audience is *involved* in a purchase decision, it has the motivation and the ability to process messages about that decision. The elaboration likelihood model (see Chapter 8) suggests that arguments should be used when an audience has the motivation and the ability to process them. In such a situation, the audience is looking for relevant information (motivated) and has the intelligence, time, and expertise (ability) to process it. The logical use of arguments and evidence is likely to be effective. On the other hand, emotion may be effective when an audience lacks the motivation or the ability to process the message.

Product may be classified as either feeling or thinking.[10] *Feeling products*, such as wines or paintings, are those that are evaluated primarily by personal preference, on which two or more individuals could reasonably differ. Examples of preference attributes are taste, flavor, style, or design. In contrast, *thinking products*, such as washing machines or car batteries, are those that are purchased on reason, on which consumers are likely to agree. Examples of such reason attributes are performance, reliability, quality, or fit. Emotional appeals are preferable for feeling products, especially if people are involved in their purchase. Argument seems preferable for thinking products. However, even for these products, emotional appeals can be quite effective. For example, ads for cameras, insurance, airlines, and computer products often resort to emotional appeals.

Exhibit 10.3   Ad With Good Link Between Stimulus and Message

Mood can be defined as a transitory, generalized emotional state that is not directed at any particular object or activity. Moods can be individual based or context based. The former are unique to each individual based on the experiences and personality of that individual prior to the advertising.

Context-based moods are those that are stimulated by the environment of the ad and can be common to all individuals facing that environment. Several studies indicate that, in general, positive moods are associated with more persuasion and positive attitudes toward the ad and the brand. On the other hand, negative moods are associated with less persuasion and more negative attitudes toward the brand.[11] In addition, harmony between emotions and mood could also enhance persuasion. Thus, positive emotions are more effective in positive mood states and vice versa.[12]

As one might expect, emotional appeals are likely to work better with people who tend to be more emotional than rational. One study confirmed this expectation.[13] It found that subjects who were high on a scale measuring emotional intensity were more responsive to emotional appeals than subjects who were not so disposed. There was no difference in response to nonemotional appeals.

When considering these factors, one important issue to keep in mind is that emotion and argument do not have to be exclusive. The dichotomy between two routes to persuasion or between emotions and arguments is a pedagogical tool to aid understanding rather than a strategic choice.[14] Indeed, the explicit mode of arousing emotions described above indicates that certain vivid arguments can themselves arouse emotions. Thus, a clever ad may resort to both emotions and arguments and blend them creatively.

Methods of Arousing Emotions

How can advertisers arouse emotions? The following sections describe five methods of arousing emotions that are particularly relevant to advertisers: drama, story, demonstration, humor, and music. Drama itself is closely related to story and demonstration, and these will be discussed together.

DRAMA, STORY, AND DEMONSTRATION

What exactly is drama? Drama involves an interaction of one or more characters around some plot, with a minimum of narration. Characters are most engaging if they are similar to those the audience experiences. The plot is a sequence of events. Plots are most engaging if they are intense and have unpredictable but credible outcomes. The narration constitutes a third party that interprets or describes what is going on with the characters involved in the plot. An example is the voiceover in a TV ad. It interferes with the spell that the drama casts on the audience.

One way to understand the role of drama is to relate it to argument, demonstration, and story.[15] The structure of these four forms of communication depends on their use of these three components of communication:

Appeal	Component		
	Narration	Plot	Characters
Argument	Yes	No	No
Demonstration	Yes	Yes	No
Story	Yes	Yes	Yes
Drama	No	Yes	Yes

Exhibit 10.4   Drama, Story, Demonstration, and Argument

SOURCE: Deighton, John, Daniel Romer, and Josh McQueen (1989), "Using Drama to Persuade," *Journal of Consumer Research*, 16 (December), 335-343. Reprinted with permission of the University of Chicago Press.

narration, plot, and characters (see Exhibit 10.4).[16] At one extreme, argument has narration but no plot or characters. At the other extreme, drama has plot and characters but no narration. Story and demonstration lie in between.

How does emotion persuade in contrast to argument? Argument relies primarily on logic with minimal feeling. Drama is the most captivating and relies primarily on emotion without necessarily relying on logic. Argument holds the viewer apart and presents him or her with the evidence. Drama draws the viewer into the action with the characters that are engaged in a plot. When successful, argument persuades a viewer by the force of the logic and the weight of the evidence; feeling is not necessary and may even be perceived as tainting the "objectivity" of the evidence. In contrast, when a drama is successful, a viewer gets lost in the plot and identifies with the feelings of the characters. Logic is not necessary and may drain the emotions. This distinction between argument and drama explains the different mechanisms by which each is effective.

Story and demonstration lie in between argument and drama. Across these four forms of persuasion, there is a tradeoff between evidence and emotion. As a communicator goes from argument, to story, demonstration, and drama, he or she relies less on logic and more on emotions.

If an advertiser wants to arouse strong emotions, then drama, story, and demonstration may be the most effective means, in that order. However, humor and music are two other means of arousing less strong emotions.

HUMOR

Consider the Coke ad in Exhibit 10.5A. Coke aired that ad in Bangkok when Michael Jackson canceled a performance after he was accused of child

Exhibit 10.5A   Humor in Advertising: An Ad With Caustic Humor

molestation in the United States. The performance was one in a tour sponsored by Pepsi. Many commentators doubted that Jackson's excuse of dehydration was genuine. (Indeed some weeks later he canceled his tour citing drug addiction.) Coke's ad is satirical with biting humor. It brings out the incongruity of a Pepsi endorser suffering from dehydration on a Pepsi-sponsored tour. Coke withdrew the ad after complaints from Pepsi and Jackson fans.

Perhaps, because of such risks, advertising experts at one time have cautioned against humor. Others think it is frivolous. For example, Claude Hopkins, "a grandfather of modern advertising, asserted that 'frivolity has no place in advertising.'"[17] However, advertisers continue to use humor in advertising. Reports indicate that humor constituted 36% of TV ads in the United Kingdom and 24% of TV ads, 31% of radio ads, and 15% of magazine ads in the United States.[18] Indeed, humor might well be one of the most important means of arousing emotions and persuading consumers, in diverse countries and cultures.[19] What is humor? Why should advertisers use it? When and how should advertisers use it?

What Is Humor?

Humor is an elusive entity. It is easy to spot and enjoy, often triggering instantaneous laughter. But it is difficult to analyze and may evaporate on

"Before I'll ride with a drunk, I'll drive myself." —Stevie Wonder

Driving after drinking, or riding with a driver who's been drinking, is a big mistake. Anyone can see that.

Exhibit 10.5B   Humor in Advertising: An Ad With Self-Deprecating Humor

analysis. Humor may be defined as painless incongruity. The essential element of humor is the incongruity between two elements that the communicator brings together. The response from the audience is first one of surprise because the unison of the two elements is unexpected and unusual. The less the audience can guess the impending incongruity, the greater the surprise, and thus the greater the humor.

Different forms of incongruity give rise to different types of humor. Thus, self-deprecation arises from incongruity between one's own goals or image and achievements (see Exhibit 10.5B), parody arises from incongruity between an

Exhibit 10.6   A PETA Ad Parodying the Milk Ad Campaign

original and a new context (see Exhibit 10.6),[20] satire from incongruity between claims and practice (see Exhibit 10.5A), pun from incongruity of a word with two meanings (see Exhibit 10.7A), and resonance from incongruity between words and pictures in an ad (see Exhibit 10.8). The term *resonance* is used because the play of word and picture creates an echo or multiplication of meaning.[21] Resonance is a form of humor that probably occurs more often in advertising than in literature. Indeed, some authors consider resonance to be advertising's unique contribution to literary form.[22]

A. Potentially enjoyable by all consumers

On a tow truck, "We don't charge an arm and a leg. We want *tows*."
On a pizza shop window: "7 days without pizza makes one *weak*."
On a podiatrist's office, "Time wounds all *heels*."
On a tire shop window, "Invite us to your next *blowout*."
On a door of a computer store, "Out for a quick *byte*."

B. Potentially offensive to some or all consumers

A plumber, "We repair what your husband fixed."
In a restaurant window, "Don't stand there and be hungry. Come in and get fed up."
At a car dealership, "The best way to get back on your feet—miss a car payment."
At an optometrist's office, "If you don't see what you are looking for, you've come to the right place."
On an electrician's truck, "We remove your shorts."

Exhibit 10.7   Humor in Ad Headlines and Taglines

We need to differentiate slapstick humor from sophisticated humor. Slapstick humor uses a simple means to incongruity, typically by putting together two incongruous images. This approach creates little tension and requires minimal thought to appreciate. So it appeals to the less sophisticated. Sophisticated humor first builds an expectation of a certain meaning, then surprises by providing an unexpected meaning that fits equally well. The incongruity in meanings requires mental effort to resolve while the surprise and mental effort increase the pleasure.[23]

Why Must Humor Be Painless?

In addition to incongruity, the other essential component of humor is that of painlessness. If the incongruity is painful, then it ceases to be enjoyable or funny. The challenge is that what is enjoyable to one group is often painful to another.

For example, when former mayor of New York Rudy Giuliani announced he had prostate cancer, PETA ran a one-page ad, with the mayor sporting a milk mustache and the tagline "Got Prostate Cancer?" (studies at that time were linking milk consumption with prostate cancer) (see Exhibit 10.6). The ad parodied two famous symbols of ad campaigns for milk, the headline "Got Milk?" and the milk mustache. Some New Yorkers who did not like the mayor or the exploitation of cows for milk may have found the ad hilarious. However, many New Yorkers were outraged by the attempt to poke fun at a person with an illness.

Similarly, Coke's ad (see Exhibit 10.5A) can offend Jackson fans, loyal Pepsi drinkers, or athletes who often suffer from dehydration. That is why Coke withdrew the ad after complaints of insensitivity from Pepsi. Ethnic

Exhibit 10.8   An Example of Resonance in Ads

jokes, which at one time were common in advertising, are another case. They poke fun at a minority by exaggerating the latter's known idiosyncrasies. The jokes may entertain a majority but are painful to that ethnic group and to those who empathize with the group. For advertisers, the incongruity has to be painless not only to the majority but also to viewers nationally and internationally. In this sense, a safe form of humor is self-deprecating humor as in Exhibit 10.5B.

Exhibit 10.7 provides a list of humorous headlines or tagline in ads. Note that some are entirely inoffensive, while others have the potential to offend one or another group in the audience. Also, notice how a slight play on words differentiates between a bland, potentially humorous and potentially offensive statement.

Why Does Humor Work?

Many factors contribute to humor's effectiveness.

First, humor relaxes an audience. Public speakers often start their talk with a joke. At the start, tension is high, as the audience and speaker do not know what to expect of each other. Humor tends to break the ice and establish a bond between communicator and audience.

Second, by arousing feelings of surprise and entertainment, humor puts the audience in a pleasant mood, which can transfer on to the brand, or ease the acceptance of the message.

Third, humor may also help to attract or retain attention. In the midst of many hard-sell argumentative ads, or others with routine appeals, humor can provide a welcome diversion.

Fourth, as with drama and story, humor may also serve as a digression that distracts the viewer's attention and reduces his or her resistance to the central message. The resistance arises from counterarguments to any direct appeal by argument.

Fifth, various forms of humor provide a small intellectual puzzle. The audience has to make an effort to solve the tension created by the double meaning as in the examples above. The solution leads to satisfaction, which may transfer on to the brand. Also, the mental effort, albeit small, is likely to help assimilation and recall of the message, or at least the brand name.[24]

Thus, humor has several factors in its favor.

When and How to Use Humor

Indiscriminate use of humor may do more to hinder than help the acceptance of the message. Several factors need to be kept in mind to use humor effectively.

First, as emphasized above, a feeling of joy or pleasure is an essential component of humor. For this reason, advertisers must avoid humor that hurts, ridicules, or in some way offends one or another group in the audience.[25]

Second, surprise arising from incongruity is an essential component of humor.[26] However, this incongruity needs to be carefully tailored to the audience. Trivial incongruity to a sophisticated audience may cause the incongruity to appear slapstick. On the other hand, sophisticated incongruity for a simple audience may cause it to appear obscure. Similarly, incongruity may not work if it appears unbelievable or unrelated to the message or an audience.[27]

Third, brevity helps. It can enhance the element of surprise and add punch to humor. Long-winded stories or explanations can kill humor.

Fourth, the emotional context of the audience also affects humor. In a very serious or tense moment, a mild form of humor may provoke much joy; in a sad or sorrowful occasion, the same humor may be offensive.

Fifth, some research indicates that humor is more suited for some types of products than for others. In particular, some authors argue that, because of its lighter approach to persuasion, humor is more suited for low-priced, less risky products (e.g., detergents, coffee) and among these, for more expressive or feeling products.[28]

Sixth, the social context of humor can affect its enjoyment. Research indicates that humor is funnier when it occurs in a string of humorous episodes than when it occurs alone. Also, the sight or sound of a social group enjoying jokes increases an individual's enjoyment of the same.[29] Thus, humor during programs such as major sporting events, which are generally viewed in groups, is likely to be specially enjoyed, and probably more effective than at other times.

MUSIC

Music can grab attention, as a sudden burst of harmony; it can linger in memory as a catchy jingle.[30] It can accentuate certain visual or dramatic elements of an ad.[31] Music may even add meanings to the ad.[32] But the most important and common use of music is to establish mood or arouse emotions.[33] Examples include music played at important life occasions, at religious and spiritual events, during various forms of entertainment, and for numerous forms of promotion. The use of music for the latter purpose is pervasive. One study of 1,000 TV commercials found that music was present in 42% of the ads and explicitly carried the message in 12%.[34]

The Effects of Music on Emotions and Behavior

What is music? How does it affect our emotions? There is a variety of music originating in different countries, cultures, epochs, and styles. Yet permutations and combinations of three important elements (pitch, timing, and texture) form all of these different forms of music.[35] Pitch is the organization of notes in a musical piece. Timing is the temporal organization of the components of the piece. Texture describes the qualitative richness of the musical piece. These components are important because research has shown that each of them affects mood and emotions in different ways.

What Emotions Does Music Arouse?

Research in music, anthropology, and other disciplines has tried to calibrate the precise emotions aroused by the different components of music. Some results may be commonly known. For example, a sentimental piece tends to be slow, flowing, and soft; a triumphant piece tends to be loud and fast. What is less well known is that the elements of music may be associated with specific emotions. Exhibits 10.9 and 10.10 summarize some findings from a review of past research.[36] For example, a promoter wishing to amplify the serenity of a scene should choose music that is slow, flowing, and soft as one may intuitively suggest, but also one that has medium pitch, consonant harmony, and a major mode.[37] Such music would differ from one that is sentimental in only one, important way; sentimental music would preferably be in minor mode, while serene music would be in major mode. Musicians who create music for a promoter probably do so on the basis of aesthetics and fit with the context of the ad. However, Exhibits 10.9 and 10.10 can be a valuable guide for managers to ensure that the music meets their goals. In addition, the exhibits list precise emotional expressions that go with various musical components.

What Behaviors Does Music Affect?

Music at the point of purchase is very common and is often chosen to establish special moods. However, the effects of music on behavior have not been as well researched as those on emotions. One study found that slow background music in a restaurant increased the average time spent in the restaurant to 56 minutes compared to 45 minutes when fast music was played. The patrons also spent 36% more on drinks with slow music rather than fast music ($30 instead of $22).[38] The authors of that study argued that slow music was more relaxing and encouraged a more leisurely pace. But because the amount of food that can be consumed is limited by physical and etiquette constraints, the patrons spent more on drinks. In a similar vein, another study found that slow music slowed down the in-store traffic flow and increased the sales volume compared to fast music.[39] These studies indicate that the components of music such as tempo can affect behavior. It would be interesting to find out if the other components of music also have similar effects on various behaviors.

Are the Effects of Music in Humans Instinctive or Learned?

Research on this issue has not come to a consensus. The answer is probably both, with some very basic aspects being instinctive and subtle aspects being learned within the context of a culture or subculture. For example, sudden, loud sounds tend to frighten newborn animals and humans even if they have

Emotional Expression

Musical Element	Serious	Sad	Sentimental	Serene	Humorous	Happy	Exciting	Majestic	Frightening
Mode	Major	Minor	Minor	Major	Major	Major	Major	Major	Minor
Tempo	Slow	Slow	Slow	Slow	Fast	Fast	Fast	Medium	Slow
Pitch	Low	Low	Medium	Medium	High	High	Medium	Medium	Low
Rhythm	Firm	Firm	Flowing	Flowing	Flowing	Flowing	Uneven	Firm	Uneven
Harmony	Consonant	Dissonant	Consonant	Consonant	Consonant	Consonant	Dissonant	Dissonant	Dissonant
Volume	Medium	Soft	Soft	Soft	Medium	Medium	Loud	Loud	Varied

Exhibit 10.9   Role of Music in Arousing Emotions

SOURCE: Developed primarily from Hevner (1937), Kinnear (1959), and Vinovich (1975) with additional information from Gundlach (1935), Sherer and Oshinsky (1977), Watson (1942), and Wedlin (1972) , as reported in Bruner, Gordon C., II (1990), "Music, Mood, and Marketing," *Journal of Marketing*, 54, 4 (October), 94–104. Reprinted with permission of the American Marketing Association.

Time-Related Expressions

1. Duple rhythms produce a rigid and controlled expression in comparison with triple rhythms, which are more relaxed or abandoned.

2. The faster the tempo, the more animation and happiness is expressed.

3. Even, rhythmic movement can represent the unimpeded flow of some feeling; dotted, jerky, uneven rhythms produce more complex expressions.

4. Firm rhythms suggest a serious mood whereas smooth-flowing rhythms are more playful.

5. Staccato notes give more emphasis to a passage than legato notes.

Pitch-Related Expressions

1. "Up" and "down" in pitch not only correspond to up and down in the physical world but can also imply "out-and-in" as well as "away-and-back," respectively.

2. Rising and falling pitch can convey a growing or diminishing intensity in a given emotional context.

3. Songs in higher keys are generally considered to be happier than songs in lower keys.

4. Music in the major mode expresses more animated and positive feelings than music in the minor mode.

5. Complex harmonies are more agitated and sad than simple harmonies, which are more serene and happy.

Texture-Related Expressions

1. Loudness can suggest animation or proximity whereas low volume implies tranquility or distance.

2. Crescendo (soft to loud) expresses an increase in force whereas diminuendo (loud to soft) suggests a decrease in power.

3. The timbre of brass instruments conveys feeling of cold, hard force whereas reed instruments produce a lonely, melancholy expression.

Exhibit 10.10   Emotional Expressions of Music

SOURCE: Bruner, Gordon C., II (1990), "Music, Mood, and Marketing," *Journal of Marketing,* 54, 4 (October), 94-104. Reprinted with permission of the American Marketing Association.

prior experience of them.[40] This response may be one that evolved to protect the species. Also, the findings listed in Exhibits 10.9 and 10.10 may hold across cultures, suggesting some universal human responses to music.[41] At the same time, some researchers argue strongly that music is a rich and complex form of human expression that derives its meaning only from a culture. According to this view, one has to "learn" to appreciate music and to associate various meanings and emotions with it.[42] Furthermore, because familiar forms of music tend to be associated with specific stories, events, and emotions (e.g., pop songs, the national anthem), they may each evoke a set of unique meanings and emotions. For example, a Christmas carol may put shoppers in a Christmas mood, which they may associate with happy holidays, joyful gifts, relaxing winter activities, and warm family time.

The cultural interpretation of music has two important implications for promoters. First, the findings of Exhibits 10.9 and 10.10 must be applied carefully in an international context, because most of them have been derived with studies in Western culture. Second, choosing a new piece may be better than a well-known piece for specific ads. A well-known piece may arouse instant recognition, liking, and emotions, but some of these emotions may not be consistent with the promoter's goals. An original composition may not have instant appeal or recall, but careful design and repetition in a campaign may render it an effective means to arouse strong emotions and loyalty to a brand.

When Are the Effects of Music Likely to Be Most Important?

As suggested by the elaboration likelihood model, the effect of music is likely to be more important when viewers use a peripheral route of persuasion based on cues. In such situations, one study suggests that emotion-arousing music can increase the attention of viewers while message-related music can enhance their processing of the message.[43]

However, the same study suggests that music may also help when viewers use a central route. Message-related music increases such viewers' attention to the message while it also positively affects their emotions. Emotion-arousing music positively affects the emotions of such viewers, though it might distract them from processing the message.

Role of Specific Emotions

Advertisers arouse some emotions more often than others, either intentionally as part of their strategy or unintentionally due to the product, execution, or timing of the ad. These emotions include irritation, warmth, fear, and inspiration or ennobling emotions. There has also been more research trying to understand the role of these emotions than that of other emotions. This chapter reviews this literature next.

IRRITATION

Consider the following two examples:

A Stayfree ad opens with two professional models running to catch a taxi. The taxi driver turns out to be an attractive female. Once in the taxi, the established model tells the younger model and the taxi driver in detail about

Stayfree maxi pads. She then pulls out a package to demonstrate the product attributes.

A Tylenol ad shows a mother in obvious discomfort describing the onset of a headache. She points to where it starts and where it moves. She claims that her two boys are usually the headache's cause and she was mean to them. She then takes Tylenol and enjoys quick relief from her symptoms.[44]

Many readers may find these ads irritating. That is a common emotion aroused by advertising today. One cause for irritation may be that much advertising today is intrusive. People receive ads through TV, radio, newspapers, magazines, mail, phone, and the Internet, often when they do not expect, need, or want them. But even then advertising need not be irritating; it could be stimulating, entertaining, and enjoyable. The key questions we need to address are the following: Why are ads like the ones above irritating? Is irritating advertising less effective? How common is irritation?

Level of Irritation

At least two studies, one in the mid-1960s and the other around 1985, examined the issue of irritation in advertising.[45] The results from both studies are similar. The latter study surveyed the responses of 1,000 households to 524 prime-time TV commercials. The study found that on average 6% of the respondents rated as irritating the commercials that they recognized. In comparison, the rating for silly was 7%, for amusing 13%, and for informative 18%. Thus overall, irritating does not seem to be a dominant emotion aroused by ads. However, the cause for irritation was not random; it came from certain distinct features of the ad.

Causes of Irritation

Exhibit 10.11 shows the mean rating of irritation by type of ad and product category. Two points are evident in this exhibit. First, irritation is strongly influenced by product category. Notice especially that ads for products for feminine hygiene, hemorrhoids, and laxatives score consistently higher on irritation. Second, there is a difference within categories by brand and by execution of the same brand. For example, Massengill scores 36, Stayfree scores 33, while New Freedom scores 22. Thus, proper execution can mitigate the irritation that would normally be aroused by a product, while poor execution may increase it.

The authors of the study content analyzed the ads to find out what specific execution factors were responsible for irritation. They identified nine factors that are here organized into three groups: illustration, plot, and characterization.

	Sample Size	Total Irritation
Feminine Hygiene Average		29
Massengill	278	36
Stayfree	367	33
Kotex	305	30
Kotex	294	29
Stayfree	353	29
OB tampons	348	27
Tampax	330	26
New Freedom	339	22
Hemorrhoid and Laxative Average		18
Preparation H	323	20
Phillips	326	19
Phillips	279	17
Preparation H	356	15
Women's Undergarments Average		16
Playtex bra	255	18
Playtex bra	409	15
Playtex briefs	351	15
Soap/Bleach Average		16
Clorox	373	16
All	258	16

(Continued)

Exhibit 10.11 (Continued)

	Sample Size	Total Irritation
Palmolive	441	15
Misc. Drug Products Average		16
Pepto-Bismol	323	18
Colgate	325	17
Scope	416	17
Rolaids	489	16
Arthritis Pain	324	16
Aim	370	16
Listerine	367	16
Fabrege	325	15
Right Guard	407	16
Tums	437	15
Overall average		19

Exhibit 10.11   The Most Irritating Commercials

SOURCE: Adapted from Aaker, David A., and Donald A Bruzzone (1985), "Causes of Irritation in Advertising," *Journal of Marketing*, 49 (Spring), 47-57. Reprinted with permission of the American Marketing Association.

Illustration. The ad explicitly shows the picture, use, or effect of a sensitive product (e.g., absorbent power of Stayfree). The ad shows a graphic, detailed demonstration of discomfort (e.g., pain from hemorrhoids or headaches).

Plot. The situation in the ad is contrived, phony, unbelievable, or overdramatized (e.g., quick response with Tylenol). The tension from the plot is uncomfortable (e.g., two professional women discussing Stayfree). The ad includes a suggestive scene.

Characterization. The ad "puts down" a character in terms of appearance, knowledge, or sophistication (mother berates a child for choosing a toothpaste on a wrong criterion, taste.). The ad involves a threat to an important relationship such as parent-child, husband-wife, or close friend (e.g., a wife threatens to quit a husband's bed if he sneezes once more). The casting of a character is poor.

Compared to product and execution, demographics do not appear to be a major factor influencing irritation. Nonusers tend to be more irritated by ads for the product than are users of a product. But surprisingly, for feminine hygiene, the levels of irritation do not vary by user group. Thus, product sensitivity and execution are critical factors for this category. There were small differences by gender and socioeconomic groups. Irritation was higher among white-collar, more highly educated, and upper-income consumers. It was a little higher among men than among women.

Effectiveness of Irritating Ads

Two theories address the issue of how irritation aroused by an ad affects response to the ad. One theory suggests a simple monotonic response: Higher irritation leads to increasing dislike of the ad and the brand advertised. The reason could be conditioning, whereby repeated association causes irritation with the ad to transfer to the brand, or selectivity, whereby viewers pay less attention to ads they find irritating.

Another theory suggests a "check-mark-shaped" curve between ad response and the emotional appeal of the ad.[46] The left arm of the check mark arises from irritating ads probably being more effective than neutral ones. The higher positive response of irritating ads compared to neutral ones may be because irritation heightens attention and recall of the message while distracting from counterarguments. As a result, the respondent is more likely to remember the brand and its attributes and choose it over its rivals. The right arm of the check mark arises because ads that arouse a positive emotion such as warmth are more effective than both neutral ones and those that are irritating. Warm ads probably have all the attention-gaining and recall benefits of irritating ads while they also transfer a positive emotion to the product.

Which of these two theories is correct is still an open matter. Some studies using print ads in laboratory experiments seem to support the first theory, while others support the second. In either case, advertisers need to consider arousing warmth as frequently if not more often than arousing irritation.

WARMTH

While irritating ads may still be effective, intentionally developing irritating ads may be risky. A better strategy may be to use warmth in advertising because of the check-mark-shaped response discussed above. Warmth may have the same attention and recall advantages of irritation, but may be even more effective in persuasion for the brand and message.[47] The reason is that warmth relaxes viewers and puts them in a positive frame of mind. Through adequate repetitions this feeling can transfer to the brand and message, enhancing persuasion.

Warmth may be a background feeling that is the by-product of a carefully crafted ad, or it may be a primary purpose of an ad. It can be stimulated by pictures or stories of love, friendship, caring, or tenderness among humans or animals. Scenes of peace, tranquility, and harmony among people, animals, and nature can also stimulate warmth. Besides positive relations and nature, humor and music can also promote an atmosphere of warmth to aid the persuasiveness of the ad.

FEAR

Consider the following example:

A TV ad for First Alert, a carbon monoxide detector, shows pictures of real people enjoying life. Each of their loved ones then tells how they died of carbon monoxide poisoning. Besides the fear of death, the ad evokes the guilt of the survivor, who could have prevented the accident with First Alert.[48]

Fear is a common emotion that ads arouse today, and it may be on the rise.[49] Fear seems more relevant to a particular class of products—those dealing with health and safety. Thus, it seems natural to develop fear appeals against drug abuse, alcoholism, unsafe driving, unsafe sex, unsafe houses, or lack of insurance, to name some examples. A person unfamiliar with the problems of addiction is likely to suggest a strong ad campaign that vividly portrays the dangers of the unhealthy or unsafe practice. He or she believes that arousing intense fear is likely to generate immediate and sustained compliance with the desired behavior.

Nature of Response to Fear

However, various segments of the population may respond differently to different fear appeals, such as loss of life, family, or financial status.[50] For example, some consumers might not drink and drive for fear of being arrested, while others might not do so for fear of an accident, and still others might refrain from the practice for fear of hurting others.[51]

Moreover, the response to fear is not necessarily linear. In simple words, greater fear does not necessarily mean greater compliance.[52] A large number of studies tried to determine how consumers respond to fear. While the results of these studies are not completely in agreement, there is some rationale for an inverted-U-shaped response to fear.[53] That is, response increases as we go from no fear to a moderate level of fear. But it begins to decrease again as we move from moderate fear to strong fear. The reason is that a little fear may be ignored, but extreme fear may prompt a defense reaction. In the latter situation, viewers may dismiss the stimulus as exaggerated, dismiss the evidence as unscientific, or just screen out the entire ad to protect them from the pain of viewing it. As a result, the fear appeal may boomerang, promoting no response to the message or even a hardening of the original position.

Besides preventing defense reactions, moderate fear may also be more effective, because some understatement may prompt the viewer to do more of the thinking on the issue. Thus, a clever fear appeal is to suggest the danger of noncompliance as mildly as possible while stressing the advantage of compliance. Mixing warmth, surprise, or humor with or instead of fear can be quite effective, as the next two examples illustrate. The U.S. Department of Transportation uses the warm, smiling faces of victims of drunk driving accidents to arouse sorrow at this avoidable loss. Michelin uses the cuddly, smiling faces of babies to remind parents of the importance of good, safe tires.

Another subtle use of fear is to build a story or drama where the message is not clear until the last line, by which time the viewer is unable to build a defense mechanism. A clever use of fear is to mix it with humor. Instead of emphasizing the dangers of noncompliance, the ad can joke about it.

ENNOBLING EMOTIONS

Ennobling emotions are those that inspire audiences to difficult action with feelings such as pride, courage, or dedication. Products where such appeals may be more effective are professions in which the salary is low while the apparent costs are high. Example are the military, public service, teaching, or religious life. What motivates people to adopt these professions? One important factor may be affinity for the work involved in these professions. A more important factor may be the intangible satisfaction derived from performing a "service" even though, or precisely because, it is not rewarded adequately in monetary terms. For example, what price can one put on getting maimed in defense of one's country? How can one measure the joy of reading to the blind, teaching a child, or giving someone peace of mind? The deeper rewards of these professions are thus intangible, subjective, and not based on price.

Promotions for these professions then can adopt one of the two routes to persuasion discussed above, argument or emotion. They can use argument to emphasize the tangible merits of adopting the profession. For example, the army's campaign "Be all you can be" stressed the training in the army that lets you attain your fullest potential at the army's cost. However, the use of emotions may be the more powerful route to fire the minds of those who adopt these professions. Story and drama seem to be the best methods to adequately tap such emotions.

Culture may be an important factor that determines the success of the appeal of pride. One study found that an ego-focused appeal such as pride was more effective than an other-focused appeal such as empathy in more individualist cultures compared to collectivist cultures.[54] Another study found that, when appealing for help or donations, pity was more effective than pride. The reason is that consumers are more likely to give to an underdog out of pity rather than to a winner who is already doing fine.[55]

The examples above show how the lives and motives of members of the profession can be used to develop inspirational ads for new recruits. However, Nike showed that the arousal of ennobling emotions need not be restricted to the professions. It could also be aroused for athletic goods, where the cost of training can also be steep and the benefits are not always immediate or tangible. For these campaigns, Nike adopted several approaches.

One approach imbued the drama and intensity of athletic activity into the personality of the shoes. For example, in one spot quick cuts of athletes in various dramatic episodes gripped viewers' attention, while a final shot of Nike associated these feelings with the brand name. Another approach was less explicit. It emphasized self-actualization with the theme "Just do it." Various stories or mini-dramas portrayed the challenges of daily life and the need for consumers to take a stand and make the tough choices. A third approach lay in between these two strategies. It consisted of a series of four two-page ads for women's shoes.

The power of these ads is in the copy, which is part story, part deep empathy with a woman's athletic challenges, and part inspirational homily. This campaign of Nike's was very successful. One ad caused Nike's switchboard to be jammed. Women called up to indicate how the ad changed their lives or convinced them that Nike really understood a woman's feelings. Overall, the campaign generated 110,000 phone calls in 6 months and fueled a 24% growth in sales of women's shoes.[56]

Summary

While the elaboration likelihood model principally contrasts the role of arguments versus cues in persuasion, the framework can also explain the roles of some other variables involved in persuasion, particularly emotion, humor, mood, and music.[57] These variables are important primarily in the peripheral route to persuasion although they could play a supporting role to arguments in the central route. For instance, while the use of emotions could enhance the effect of strong arguments in the central route, emotions can be the sole means of persuasion in the peripheral route. Similarly, while humor can ease the resistance to a strong argument in the central route, in the peripheral route it may persuade by merely generating goodwill to the brand. The same can be said for the other two variables, music and mood. Some authors have suggested that the role of emotions may be more complex than that described above, because emotions can propel message receivers into a state of higher involvement. Emotions can also lead to immediate action more effectively than can reason. Graphic images of the killing of baby seals to harvest their coats served both to raise the public's involvement in this environmental issue and to motivate an immediate change in the public's demand for clothes made of seals' coats.

Notes

1.   For example, see Batra, Rajeev, and Michael L. Ray (1986), "Affective Responses Mediating Acceptance of Advertising," *Journal of Consumer Research*, 13, 2 (September), 234-249; Holak, Susan L., and William J. Havlena (1998), "Feelings, Fantasies and Memories: An Examination of the Emotional Components of Nostalgia," *Journal of Business Research*, 42 (July), 217-226.

2.   For a slightly different typology, see Deighton, John, and Stephen J. Hoch (1993), "Teaching Emotion With Drama Advertising," in *Advertising Exposure, Memory, and Choice*, Andrew A. Mitchell (ed.). Hillsdale, NJ: Lawrence Erlbaum.

3.   Stern, Barbara B. (1994), "Classical and Vignette Television Advertising Dramas: Structural Models, Formal Analysis and Consumer Effects," *Journal of Consumer Research*, 20 (March), 601-615.

4.   Stern, "Classical and Vignette."

5.   Ambler, Tim, and Tom Burne (1999), "The Impact of Affect on Memory of Advertising," *Journal of Advertising Research*, 39, 2 (March-April), 25-34; Stewart, David W., Kenneth M. Farmer, and Charles I. Stannard (1990), "Music as a Recognition Cue in Advertising—Tracking Studies," *Journal of Advertising Research* (August-September), 39-48.

6.   Steadman, Major (1969), "How Sexy Illustrations Affect Brand Recall," *Journal of Advertising Research*, 9 (March), 15-19.

7.   Percy, Larry, and John R. Rossiter (1992), "Advertising Stimulus Effects: A Review," *Journal of Current Issues and Research in Advertising*, 14, 1 (Spring), 75-90.

8.   Smith, Martin J. (1992), "Designing a Dispute," *Orange County Register*, February 14, 1.

9.   Kamp, Edward, and Deborah J. MacInnis (1995), "Characteristics of Portrayed Emotions in Commercials," *Journal of Consumer Research* (November/December), 19-26.

10.   Ratchford, Brian (1987), "New Insights About the FCB Grid," *Journal of Advertising Research*, 27, 4 (August/September), 31. FCB is an acronym for Foote, Cone and Belding.

11.   Gardner, Meryl P. (1993), "Responses to Emotional and Informational Appeals: The Moderating Role of Context-Induced Mood States," in *Attention, Attitude and Affect in Response to Advertising*, Eddie M. Clark, Timothy C. Brock, and David W. Stewart (eds.), Hillsdale, NJ: Lawrence Erlbaum; Goldberg, Marvin E., and Gerald J. Gorn (1987), "Happy and Sad TV Programs: How They Affect Reactions to Commercials," *Journal of Consumer Research*, 14 (December), 387-403.

12.   Cunningham, Michael, Jeff Steinberg, and Rita Grev (1980), "Wanting to and Having to Help: Separate Motivation for Positive Mood and Guilt-Induced Helping," *Journal of Personality and Social Psychology*, 38 (2), 181-192.

13.   Moore, David J., William D. Harris, and Hong C. Chen (1995), "Affect Intensity. An Individual Difference Response to Advertising Appeals," *Journal of Consumer Research*, 22, 2 (September), 154-165.

14.   Meenaghan, Tony (1995), "The Role of Advertising in Brand Image Development," *Journal of Product and Brand Management*, 4, 4, 23-34.

15.   Deighton, John, Daniel Romer, and Josh McQueen (1989), "Using Drama to Persuade," *Journal of Consumer Research*, 16 (December), 335-343. The subsequent section draws ideas and propositions from this article.

16.   Deighton et al., "Using Drama to Persuade."

17.   McQuarrie, Edward F., and David Glen Mick (1992), "On Resonance: A Critical Pluralistic Inquiry Into Advertising Rhetoric," *Journal of Consumer Research*, 19 (September), 180-197.

18.   Weinberger, Marc G., Harlan Spotts, Leland Campbell, and May L. Parsons (1995), "The Use and Effect of Humor in Different Advertising Media," *Journal of Advertising Research* (May/June), 44-56; Weinberger, Marc, and Harlan Spotts (1989), "Humor in U.S. Versus U.K. TV Advertising," *Journal of Advertising*, 18, 2, 39-44; Weinberger, Marc G., and Leland Campbell (1990-1991), "The Use and Impact of Humor in Radio Advertising," *Journal of Advertising Research* (December-January), 44-51; McQuarrie and Mick, "On Resonance."

19.   De Pelsmacker, Patrick, and M. Geuens (1998), "Reactions to Different Types of Ads in Belgium and Poland," *International Marketing Review*.

20.   Zinkhan, George M., and Madeline Johnson (1994), "The Use of Parody in Advertising," *Journal of Advertising*, 23 (3), (September), iii-viii.

21.   McQuarrie and Mick, "On Resonance." Some examples and ideas from this section are also drawn from this article.

22.   Sheldon, Esther K. (1956), "Some Pun Among the Hucksters," *American Speech*, 31, 13-20.

23.   Zhang, Yong (1996), "Responses to Humorous Advertising: The Moderating Effect of Need for Cognition," *Journal of Advertising*, 25 (Spring), 15-32.

24.   McQuarrie and Mick, "On Resonance."

25.   Scott, Cliff, David M. Klein, and Jennings Bryant (1990), "Consumer Response to Humor in Advertising: A Series of Field Studies Using Behavioral Observation," *Journal of Consumer Research*, 16 (March), 498-501; Alden, Dana L., and Wayne D. Hoyer (1993), "An Examination of Cognitive Factors Related to Humorousness in Television Advertising," *Journal of Advertising*, 22, 2 (June), 29-37.

26.   Alden, Dana L, Ashesh Mukherjee, and Wayne D. Hoyer (2000), "The Effects of Incongruity, Surprise, and Positive Moderators on Perceived Humor in Television Advertising," *Journal of Advertising* (July), 1-15.

27.   Lee, Yih Hwai, and Charlotte Mason (1999), "Responses to Information Incongruence in Advertising: The Role of Expectancy, Relevancy, and Humor," *Journal of Consumer Research*, 26, 2 (September), 156-169.

28.   Weinberger et al., "The Use and Effect of Humor"; Spotts, Harlan E., Marc G. Weinberger, and Amy L. Parsons (1997), "Assessing the Use and Impact of Humor on Advertising Effectiveness: A Contingency Approach," *Journal of Advertising*, 26, 3 (Fall), 17-32.

29.   Zinkhan, George, and Yong Zhang (1991), "Television Advertising: The Effects of Repetition on Social Setting," *Advances in Consumer Research* 18, 813-818.

30.   Stewart, David W., Kenneth M. Farmer, and Charles I. Stannard (1990), "Music as a Recognition Cue in Advertising-Tracking Studies," *Journal of Advertising Research* (August-September), 39-48; Stewart, David W., and Girish Punj (1998), "Effects of Using a Nonverbal (Musical) Cue on Recall and Playback of Television Advertising: Implications for Advertising Tracking," *Journal of Business Research* (May).

31.   Hung, Kineta (2000), "Framing Meaning Perceptions With Music: The Case of Teaser Ads," *Journal of Advertising* 29 (Spring), 25-34.

32. Hung, Kineta (2000), "Narrative Music in Congruent and Incongruent TV Advertising," *Journal of Advertising,* 29, 1 (Spring), 25-34.

33. Alpert, Judy I., and Mark I. Alpert (1990), "Music Influences on Mood and Purchase Intentions," *Psychology and Marketing,* 7 (Summer), 109-134.

34. Stewart, David W., and David H. Furse (1986), *Effective Television Advertising: A Study of 1000 Commercials,* Lexington, MA: Lexington Books.

35. Bruner, Gordon C., II (1990), "Music, Mood and Marketing," *Journal of Marketing,* 54, 4 (October), 94-104. The subsequent definitions are adapted from this review of the literature on the topic.

36. Ibid.

37. *Harmony* is the simultaneous occurrence of two or more notes. Harmony that is pleasing is called *concordant,* and that which is displeasing is called *discordant. Mode* is a fixed set of notes in which a song or parts of a song are played. Western music uses one of two modes: *major* or *minor.*

38. Milliman, Ronald E. (1986), "The Influence of Background Music on the Behavior of Restaurant Patrons," *Journal of Consumer Research,* 13 (September), 286-289.

39. Milliman, Ronald E. (1982), "The Effects of Background Music Upon the Shopping Behavior of Supermarket Patrons," *Journal of Marketing,* 46, 3, 86-91.

40. Waldholz, Michael (1993), "Study of Fear Shows Emotions Can Alter 'Wiring' of the Brain," *Wall Street Journal,* September 29, 1.

41. Bruner, "Music, Mood and Marketing."

42. Scott, Linda M. (1990), "Understanding Jingles and Needle Drop: A Rhetorical Approach to Music in Advertising," *Journal of Consumer Research,* 17 (September) 223-236; see also MacInnis, Deborah J., and C. Whan Park (1991), "The Differential Role of Characteristics of Music on High and Low Involvement Consumers' Processing of Ads," *Journal of Consumer Research,* 18 (September), 161-173.

43. MacInnis and Park, "The Differential Role."

44. Aaker, David A., and Donald E. Bruzzone (1985), "Causes of Irritation in Advertising," *Journal of Marketing,* 49 (Spring), 47-57.

45. Bauer, Raymond A., and Stephen A. Greyser (1968), *Advertising in America: The Consumer View,* Boston, MA: Harvard University Press; Aaker and Bruzzone, "Causes of Irritation in Advertising."

46. Aaker and Bruzzone, "Causes of Irritation in Advertising"; see also Stapel, Jan (1994), "Observations: A Brief Observation About Likeability and Interestingness of Advertising," *Journal of Advertising Research,* 34, 2 (March/April), 79-80.

47. Aaker, David A., Douglas M. Stayman, and Michael R. Hagerty (1986), "Warmth in Advertising: Measurement, Impact and Sequence Effects," *Journal of Consumer Research,* 12 (March), 365-381.

48. Deveney, Kathleen (1993), "Marketers Exploit People's Fears of Everything," *Wall Street Journal,* November 11, B1, B5.

49. Ibid.

50. LaTour, Michael, and Herbert J. Rotfeld (1997), "There Are Threats and (Maybe) Fear-Caused Arousal: Theory and Confusion of Appeals to Fear and Fear Arousal Itself," *Journal of Advertising,* 26, 3 (Fall), 45-59; Hale, Jerold L., Robert Lemieux, and Paul A. Mongeau (1995), "Cognitive Processing of Fear-Arousing Message Content" *Communication Research* (August).

51. Lavack, Anne Marie (1997), "Fear Appeals in Social Marketing Advertising," *Dissertation Abstracts International Section A: Humanities & Social Sciences,* 58, 6A (December), 2303; Schoenbachler, Denise D., and Tommy E. Whittler (1996), "Adolescent Processing of Social and Physical Threat Communications," *Journal of Advertising,* 25 (4) (Winter).

52.   For recent examples, see Gotthoffer, Alyse Renee (2000), "Effects of Fear, Localization, and Injury Threat in Public Service Advertisements on Intention to Drink and Drive Among College Students," *Dissertation Abstracts International Section A: Humanities & Social Sciences*, 60, 9-A (April), 3185.

53.   The appropriate level of fear that gets the most positive response is likely to vary across contexts. For this reason, studies done in different contexts may not always have consistent findings. Rotfeld, Herbert J. (1988), "Fear Appeals and Persuasion: Assumptions and Errors in Advertising Research, " *Journal of Current Issues and Research in Advertising*, 11, 1 & 2, 21-40; Henthorne, Tony L., Michael S. LaTour, and Rajan Natarajan (1993), "Fear Appeals in Print Advertising: An Analysis of Arousal and Ad Response," *Journal of Advertising*, 22, 2 (June), 59-69.

54.   Aaker, Jennifer L., and Patti Williams (1998), "Empathy Versus Pride: The Influence of Emotional Appeals Across Cultures," *Journal of Consumer Research*, 25 (December), 241-261.

55.   Fisher, Robert J., and David Ackerman (1998), "The Effects of Recognition and Group Need on Volunteerism: A Social Norm Perspective," *Journal of Consumer Research*, 25 (December) 262-275.

56.   Nike's 1992 annual report.

57.   Petty, Richard E., and John T. Cacioppo (1986), *Communication and Persuasion*, New York: Springer-Verlag.

11

␣rsement in Advertising

B ritney Spears. Tiger Woods. Michael Jordan. These names are symbols
of the role of endorsers in advertising today. Indeed, firms spend millions
of dollars to sign up such celebrities to endorse their products. Some brands,
such as Perdue Chicken and Norton Utilities, were built around the image
of a personality (Frank Perdue and Peter Norton, respectively). Some popular
endorsers such as Michael Jordan earn as much as $40 million a year from
endorsements alone.[1] Endorsement contracts are now so lucrative that
many professionals in sports and entertainment direct their careers to this
end. In some sports, such as track and field, winning at the Olympics has
pretty much become a means to subsequent endorsement contracts. Athletes
in demanding sports such as swimming and gymnastics are tempted to give
up the rigors of training once they win a big championship and sign up
lucrative endorsements.

Many critics bemoan the fact that advertisers rely so much on endorsers.
They point to several weaknesses of this strategy. First, many brands have a
higher consumer awareness and liking than the celebrities who endorse them.
Second, hiring endorsers, especially celebrities, is costly. Third, celebrities frequently endorse multiple brands and lack unique brand identity. Fourth,
celebrities tend to be unpredictable and can hurt brands by their behavior and
statements. Fifth, and most critical, celebrities have feet of clay. Frequently, they
get caught up in scandals that puncture their public image. For example,
Martha Stewart, Jack Welch, Kobe Bryant, Michael Jackson, and Mike Tyson
were much esteemed celebrities before some episode tarnished their image, if
not totally destroyed their reputation.

Why do advertisers use endorsers? What types should they use? When?
This chapter addresses these questions.

Types of Endorsers

Endorsers can be grouped into three classes: experts, celebrities, and lay endorsers. Each of them has special characteristics and roles in the communication process. This chapter first defines each type of endorser and then describes their role.

EXPERTS

Experts are individuals or organizations that the target population perceives as having specialized knowledge in a particular area. Examples include Venus Williams for tennis rackets and Peter Norton for Symantec's Internet Security program. Organizations may also serve as expert endorsers, in at least three different ways.[2] First, various organizations such as the American Medical, Dental, Heart, and Cancer Associations; *Good Housekeeping*; and the U.S. Department of Agriculture will certify the quality of products, sometimes through *seals of approvals*. Second, some organizations, such as J. D. Power and Associates and *Motor Trend* magazine, rate brands comparatively and allow brands to advertise such ratings. Third, some organizations allow advertisers to use qualitative descriptions of the quality of their products.

CELEBRITIES

Celebrities are individuals who are well known to the population because of the publicity associated with their lives. Celebrities may not always be explicitly identified by name, especially if they are well known to the target audience. Sometimes ads may even use celebrities as a voiceover without identification, because they are so well known. Most celebrity endorsers come from the entertainment world (Britney Spears) or the sports world (Shaquille O'Neil), though business personalities (Bill Gates) and politicians (Bob Dole) may also appear in ads. Reporters (Dan Rather), consumer advocates (Ralph Nader), and religious leaders (Jerry Falwell) could also serve as effective endorsers though they probably would be unwilling to tarnish their independence by paid commercial endorsements.

The term *celebrity* itself need not exclude individuals who are unpopular in the general population, though the latter are infrequently and selectively used as endorsers.

LAY ENDORSERS

Lay endorsers are initially unknown or fictitious individuals or characters used as spokespersons in an ad. Clever and sustained use may make them celebrities. For example, after decades of use, General Mills's Betty Crocker has become more of an expert than a lay endorser of its products.

Thus, the three types of endorsers are not mutually exclusive in practice. Some individuals could belong to more than one group depending on their reputation and the product they endorse or their reputation over time. There may be an especially large overlap between endorsers used as experts and celebrities. For example, Tiger Woods would appear for golf clubs as an expert but for Kellogg's corn flakes as a celebrity.

Why Endorsements Work

What purpose do endorsers serve in advertising today? Researchers have proposed at least three theories to explain the role of endorsers in the communication process: *source credibility theory, source attractiveness theory,* and *meaning transfer theory.* The term *source* is used here to include either an explicit endorser or, more generally, the advertiser who is a "source" of the message.

SOURCE CREDIBILITY THEORY

The source credibility theory arose from the research of social psychologists Carl Hovland and associates.[3] The central premise of the theory is that the acceptance of a message depends on the qualities of the source. Expertness and trustworthiness are two key qualities that, if present to a sufficient degree, will lead the audience to accept and internalize message.

Expertness

Expertness is the ability of the sources to make true claims. Several studies have shown that an audience will accept the claims of a source it perceives as more knowledgeable than itself on the issue. Audience acceptance increases with the expertness of the source and the inability of the audience to evaluate the product.

For example, while most computer users have heard of the Norton Antivirus program, not many know of the origin of the name. Early in 1982, when PCs were taking off, Peter Norton developed and sold a set of utilities that, among other things, helped to restore files that a user accidentally deleted. To popularize the product, he carefully cultivated an image of a PC expert by speaking to user groups, handing out tips sheets in stores, writing articles, and publishing a book. This effort was so effective that he came to be known as a PC guru. He then ran ads with his personal image and endorsement. The Norton brand became so strong that even after Symantec bought up Norton's utilities company, in 1990, Symantec still used his name on its anti-virus program.

Trustworthiness

Trustworthiness is the willingness of the source to make true claims. A source is likely to make an honest claim if it has no vested interest in the outcome or it is not under pressure to slant the evidence. Buyers would consider most advertisers to have a vested interest in stating the claims of their products. Thus, choosing an independent spokesperson in an ad helps to reduce this per-ceived bias. However, audiences generally know that spokespersons are paid. The effectiveness of the endorsement then depends on whether the audience's prior perception of the endorser as trustworthy overcomes any perceived bias that arises from the audience's knowledge of the payment.

Internalization

Persuasion through the source credibility theory is supposed to occur through a process called *internalization*. If receivers of the message find the credibility and expertness of the source acceptable, they will accept the message as the objectively correct position in this context. The receivers then integrate that message with their beliefs and the message is internalized.

SOURCE ATTRACTIVENESS THEORY

The source attractiveness theory is also based on the work of social psychologists.[4] The model posits that the acceptance of the message depends on the *attractiveness* of the source, which in turn depends on three central attributes: familiarity, likeability, and similarity. *Familiarity* is the audience's knowledge of the source through exposure, *likeability* is the affection for the source's physical appearance and behavior, and *similarity* is the resemblance between source and receiver. The better the source on each of these attributes, the more attractive it would be, and the more acceptable its message.[5] How does attractiveness affect message acceptance? At least two explanations are available: identification and conditioning.

Explanations for Source Attractiveness

Identification means that the receiver of the message begins to identify with the source because of the latter's attractiveness. In so doing, the receiver is willing to accept the opinions, beliefs, attitudes, or behavior of the source. For example, teens may adopt the dress code of a model they like very much. In contrast to the source credibility theory, the adoption of the new opinion or attitude lasts only as long as the receiver finds the source attractive. The change in identification is not as permanent as that caused by internalization. For example, a gang member probably adopts a gang's dress code through identification with other members or the gang leader. But if that member is rejected from the gang, he or she is likely to reject the dress code and other symbols of the gang.

Another explanation for the effects of source attractiveness is conditioning. *Conditioning* is a process by which affect or response to a particular source is transferred to a target by the regular association of the two stimuli. For example, by this explanation, the endorser would be the source stimulus, and the brand or product would be the target stimulus. When this endorser is repeatedly associated with the brand, the attractiveness of the former is supposed to pass on to the brand. Conditioning would also imply greater permanence in the effect of source attractiveness than identification.

Relevance of Source Attractiveness

Many empirical studies support the effectiveness of source attractiveness in eliciting a positive reaction from respondents. However, the majority of this evidence is from laboratory studies on cognitive and affective measures of response. The evidence from field studies and more behavioral measures is not as conclusive.[6] One reason might be that source attractiveness may not be as critical in advertising as the meaning transfer theory explained below.

Marketing professor Grant McCracken cites many mismatches between endorser and brand that may have derailed endorsements.[7] In all these cases, the endorsers may have been chosen based on credibility or attractiveness as the two theories described above would suggest. However, advertisers may have ignored the meanings of the endorser, which may well be the most important dimension in the choice of an endorser. While the credibility and source attractiveness models do explain some aspect of the endorsement process, the meaning transfer theory explores the complex aspect of the development and transfer of meaning.

MEANING TRANSFER THEORY

McCracken proposes meaning transfer as a richer more complete theory of the endorsement process. The central premise of the meaning transfer theory is that a celebrity encodes a unique set of meanings, which if well used can be transferred to the endorsed product. This transfer is supposed to occur in three stages (see Exhibit 11.1).

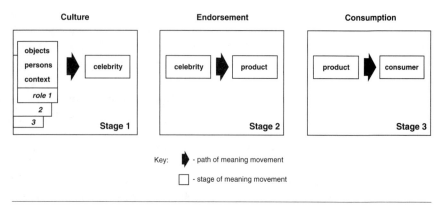

Exhibit 11.1   Meaning Transfer Model

SOURCE: Adapted from McCracken, Grant (1989), "Who Is the Celebrity Endorser? Cultural Foundations of the Endorsement Process," *Journal of Consumer Research,* 16 (December), 310-321. Copyright © 1989, The University of Chicago Press. Reprinted with permission of the University of Chicago Press.

Encoding Meanings

In the first stage, the celebrities encode a set of meanings in their image by the types of people they are, the roles they have played, and the stories that have developed around them. Each celebrity has a unique set of meanings, which can be listed by dimensions such as age, gender, race, wealth, professional status, personality, or lifestyle. However, the image of the celebrity represents this set of meanings more fully, efficiently, and effectively than any verbal listing. For example, in decades of sitcoms, Bill Cosby has played the role of a wise, witty, and warm father. As such, he makes a good spokesperson for Jell-O and would be a great endorser for a public library. On the other hand, he would be an unsuitable endorser for a Stroh's beer ad.

Meaning Transfer

In the second stage, the celebrity's skillful endorsement of the product in an ad transfers those meanings to the product. The advantage of celebrities over lay endorsers is that the celebrity encodes an image that cannot be found anywhere else, nor can it be described precisely and efficiently in the confines of an ad. When skillfully portrayed, celebrities can communicate this image more powerfully than lay endorsers or other forms of communication. For example, Britney Spears portrays sexy, youthful ebullience, which PepsiCo seeks for Pepsi Cola. The advertiser needs to evaluate all the meanings a celebrity holds, determine which if any of those meanings are desired by its target segments, and fashion a communication strategy that transfers all those meanings, and only those meanings, from the celebrity to the product.

Meaning Capture

In the third stage, consumers buy the endorsed product with the intention of capturing some of the desirable meanings with which celebrities have imbued the product. The meaning transfer theory assumes that consumers purchase products not merely for their functional value but also for their cultural and symbolic value. Typically, expensive, socially visible products would fit this category. For example, designer clothes, perfumes, premium cars, cell phones, or club memberships are often chosen more on social rather than on functional value.

In contrast to the source attractiveness and credibility models that rely on only a few key characteristics of the source, the meaning transfer theory is much richer because it focuses on a wide spectrum of meanings that can be transferred. This theory also focuses on a proper matchup of the images of the brand and the endorser. This matchup may be the most important factor to choosing an endorser.[8] However, the task is challenging and requires creativity in identifying, profiling, and selecting celebrities and skillfully using them to exploit their useful meanings for the brand.

When to Use Endorsers

Which of these three theories is the most appropriate? When should advertisers use each type of endorser? What mode of communication should the endorser use? These are pertinent questions that this chapter answers under four headings: domain of the theories, audience conditions, cost-effectiveness, and communication modes.

DOMAIN OF THE THEORIES

Each of these three models contains some aspect of the truth, and is more relevant in some circumstances. The source credibility theory is probably most relevant for explaining the role of experts as endorsers; indeed, the central concepts of the theory, expertness and trustworthiness, are defining characteristics of experts. The source attractiveness theory is probably most relevant in the case of lay endorsers; the familiarity, likeability, and similarity of these endorsers to the target audience are key to their effectiveness. The meaning transfer theory best explains the use of celebrities as endorsers; it provides an insightful framework for using the complexity of meanings associated with celebrities.

However, each of the theories has some relevance for all types of endorsers. For example, perfumes based on celebrities are often launched or are most successful at the peak of a celebrity's career. When casting a lay endorser, the image portrayed by the endorser's attributes must match the product.

		Ability to Process Information	
		High	Low
Motivation to Process Information	High	Argument	Expert
	Low	Lay	Celebrity

Exhibit 11.2   Conditions for Choice of Endorsers

AUDIENCE CONDITIONS

Which of these three types of endorsers an advertiser should use, if any at all, depends on certain underlying conditions of the audience. The elaboration likelihood model (see Chapter 8) suggests that the use of endorsements is a peripheral route of persuasion. This route is effective when the audience is not motivated or able to process a message. Using these two criteria of motivation and ability, Exhibit 11.2 suggests conditions for the preferred use of the three types of endorsements discussed above.

When the listener is both motivated to process an ad and has the ability to do so, the elaboration likelihood model suggests that strong arguments would be the best route of persuasion. For example, consider a consumer on the lookout for a new PC. If that consumer were a programmer (high motivation and ability/need), he or she would decide on reason and may be offended by an endorser in an ad for computers. If the consumer were an amateur (high motivation, low ability/need) he or she may be responsive to the endorsement by an expert. If the product were soap (low motivation, high ability/need), then a lay endorser would be appropriate; if it were cologne (low motivation, low ability/need), then a celebrity would be in order. While the recommendations in Exhibit 11.2 have not been explicitly confirmed, research provides partial support for them.[9]

COST-EFFECTIVENESS

Experts and celebrities bring a great deal of value to the endorsement process. But they also cost a lot. Indeed, the demand for sports and entertainment celebrities has grown so much that advertisers have to pay millions for a few seconds of endorsement time. In addition, most celebrities endorse multiple brands, do not stay long with one contract, and compete with many others for attention in the same product category. On top of that, celebrities sometimes lose favor with the public because of some public gaffe or revealing an embarrassing secret. Given those conditions, skillful use of lay endorsers can be less risky and quite cost-effective.

COMMUNICATION MODES

An ad may also use an endorser in different modes, depending on the context of the ad and the type of endorser. There are many modes or styles of endorsements[10] such as the following:

Explicit: "I endorse this product"
Implicit: "I use this product"
Imperative: "You use this product"
Passive: Mere appearance with the product

Experts would typically adopt the explicit mode because of the authority vested in their knowledge and the audience's conscious dependence on that knowledge. For example, the American Medical Association endorsements of some brands have generally taken this mode.

Celebrities generally adopt the passive mode because of the subtler form of persuasion involved. In this case, the celebrity has so strong an appeal for the target segment that mere association is enough to communicate the attributes of the celebrity to the brand as explained in the meaning transfer theory.

Lay endorsers generally use the implicit mode, because they have neither the credibility of experts for an explicit endorsement nor the appeal of the celebrity for a passive endorsement. The *testimonial* is a type of implicit endorsement in which the endorser describes his or her experience with the product. Testimonials featuring lay endorsers such as typical consumers of the brand are quite popular for a number of household items such as home or personal care products. The primary appeal of these ads is in the audience's identification with the spokesperson. For these reasons, advertisers should choose a reasonably attractive person but one that the average audience member can identify with in terms of demographics, lifestyle, and context.

To increase the credibility of this setting, the endorser is often presented in various modes suggesting an unrehearsed endorsement. For example, one technique would be to show the endorser using a rival brand and initially unaware of the target brand's efficacy. Another would be to show the endorser as overhearing the positive attributes of the brand in a store or public place. A third technique would be a candid interview of the endorser asking why he or she uses the brand. A fourth technique would be the use of a hidden camera in which the spokesperson goes through an experiment or interview supposedly unrehearsed and unaware of the camera. However, the extensive use of these testimonials and the audience's knowledge that all spokespersons are carefully screened and paid may diminish the efficacy of this mode of endorsement.

Strategic Implications

The theory of endorsements has several strategic implications for practitioners today: the perceptions and segmentation of consumers, and the overuse, screening, and management of endorsers.

CHOOSING ENDORSERS

A critical issue in choosing endorsers is how they may be perceived by the target audience. For example a Total Research Corporation 1991 survey indicated that some top-rated brands like Kodak obtained a perceived quality rating of 84, much above the ratings of the top celebrities like Bill Cosby, who rated around 75.[11] Why then would an advertiser use such a celebrity?

The answer lies in considering the different roles of endorsers as described by the three models above. Certain endorsers bring a package of meanings to a brand that go beyond a few characteristics such as trust or liking as measured by the standardized tests. While standardized tests can rank order celebrities on certain characteristics, they are limited in not revealing specific meanings associated with these celebrities. So test scores should not be the sole criterion for selecting celebrities.

A second issue is that overall national rankings may mask the appeal to special segments. For example, at one time, churches in the United States criticized Pepsi for choosing Madonna as a spokesperson and threatened to boycott Pepsi products because Madonna came out with a controversial video, "Like a Prayer." Her selection anyway may have seemed unwise given that her overall liking in the U.S. population was only 25% at that time. However, Madonna's appeal among teens was very high, for whom she personified liberation and sexy, youthful ebullience, meanings that teens highly valued. Thus, advertisers need to consider meaning in addition to the attractiveness and credibility of the endorser, and they need to consider these attributes with respect to the segment to which they are targeting the ad.[12]

DISCREET USE OF CELEBRITIES

In one year, Coke and Diet Coke used 27 celebrities plus 31 NFL players.[13] Why did the brand resort to so many endorsers? How many endorsers should firms use to support one brand? How many for one category? Several factors may be responsible for Coke's policy. First, the 1980s witnessed a splintering of the mass market by the proliferation of brands (e.g., diet, caffeine-free colas) and media (e.g., multiple cable TV channels). Each endorser could thus serve a unique role when appearing for each brand in each medium. Second, competition for celebrities could heat up just like competition for other resources. In that case, a firm may sign up a celebrity to preempt another firm and corner the market for such images. Alternatively, a firm may sign up celebrities to match any real or perceived advantage from the celebrities signed up by a rival. Third, firms may use the celebrity merely as an entry point to gain the attention of the audience.

A related problem is the multiple endorsements of each celebrity. For example, some celebrities endorse so many brands that the unique qualities of the celebrity's image might well be lost. For example, at one time Bill Cosby appeared in ads for Coca-Cola, Jell-O, E. F. Hutton, Kodak, and Texas Instruments.[14] Research indicates that such multiple endorsements lead to lower credibility and likeability for the endorsers and lower attitude to the brand.[15] Firms do have the option of selecting only those endorsers who have few or no brands associated with their names, or binding the celebrities to an exclusive contract not to endorse other brands. However, the celebrities with the most potential are also most in demand; the exclusive contract would cost the firm the equivalent in lost earnings to the endorser from other excluded endorsements.

Thus, the central message of the meaning transfer theory is very relevant. Firms must closely evaluate the unique meanings of a celebrity and use them discreetly to develop a unique position for their brands in consumers' minds.[16] A multiplicity of endorsers especially for the same brand in the same year, or frequent changes in endorsers or the choice of an overused endorser, can weaken the effectiveness of endorsements. The overuse of celebrities may be one reason for their declining popularity. Video Storyboard Tests Inc. tests several thousand people each year to rank the best-liked ads. In 1981, celebrity ads were much liked, claiming 7 of the top-scoring ads. But in 1989, only 2 celebrity ads made the top 20. Cartoons, animated ads, and fantasy ads were much more popular.[17]

SCREENING FOR ENDORSERS

Endorsers, especially celebrities, are human. Even celebrities such as Martha Stewart and Kobe Bryant, who at one time seemed to possess outstanding integrity, can fall in public standing. The reasons might be mistakes they make or skeletons in the closet. When these stars fall, the negative publicity associated with their names may carry over to the brands they endorse, especially for less well known brands that are heavily dependent on the image of the endorser.[18] For this reason, advertisers need to be careful in choosing endorsers by screening their history and image carefully. In addition, they should use a morals clause in the contract. Such a clause gives the advertiser the right to cancel the contract without damages should anything negative about the endorser emerge, either due to present events or undisclosed past events.

MANAGING ENDORSERS

Managing celebrity contracts is almost as important as the selection and screening of celebrities. There are three important aspects of management. First, advertisers need to ensure that celebrities are fully exploited for all the exposure and meanings that they can usefully deliver to the brand. At the same time, they need to ensure that celebrities are not overused in frequency or misused in context so that their appearances have a negative or unproductive effect on the brand. Thus, in planning celebrity ads and exposure, advertisers need to consider other appearances of the celebrity in his or her own life as well as on behalf of other products.

Second, advertisers need to involve celebrities in the planning of both the product and the ad campaign, to give celebrities a feeling of importance and to gain from their ideas and perspective. For example, in contrast to most other firms, Nike takes great care in the management of their endorsers. It involves them in designing the products. It has named buildings after them. It stands by them even when they are sidelined by injuries. And it develops and uses ad campaigns with great skill so that both brands and celebrities become household names.[19]

Third and probably most important, firms should ensure that celebrities use the products they endorse. Nothing can be so damaging to the celebrity's image and the endorsement process than the discovery that the endorser is not a genuine user of the brand. The stature of the celebrity is a major impediment in this regard. Often, celebrities believe that they live in a world of their own, with their own rules, and that endorsements are an external means of earning income, not intrinsic to their lifestyles. The meaning transfer theory, however, clearly indicates that when people respond to celebrities they hope to capture some of the meanings of the celebrity. If the celebrity does not really use the product, the magic is gone and the meaning is lost.

AVOIDING STEREOTYPES

An important consideration in the selection and portrayal of endorsers is avoidance of stereotypes. Actually, this may be the most important ethical issue in the area of endorsements. Over the past two decades, major events as well as efforts by various groups have heightened the public's sensitivity to stereotyping. Such sensitivity also spills over into advertising. Two common stereotypes that are prevalent are gender and age.

Gender Stereotypes

One of the most common criticisms of advertising is the gender stereotyping that is prevalent in contemporary ads. For example, endorsers (lay or celebrities) are typically presented as young, beautiful, and sexually attractive. Some ads go further in their stereotyping of women models. Beer ads have a long history of portraying women as sexy bimbos that reward beer drinkers for buying the advertised brand. Indeed, the macho image of beers is one of the strongest for low- to medium-priced beers. Advertisers choose such models to draw attention to their ads and to associate with their brands certain images of these models. For example, soft drink ads often portray beautiful, perfectly shaped women drinkers of their brands. In ads for its top-selling cologne, Obsession, Calvin Klein portrayed Kate Moss as a "tender, dreamy-eyed, childish" Lolita, to allude to the obsession aroused by Vladimir Nabokov's original character.[20]

However, such ads can have unfavorable effects that the advertiser may not have intended. One effect may be that male audiences are so attracted to female models that they ignore some or all of the message. A second effect may be that female audiences disbelieve the portrayal of the models and reject the message. For example, the physically perfect models that frequently appear for automobiles, soft drinks, clothes, diet medications, and health clubs may lead a viewer to suspect the model's figure to be artificially developed or portrayed. The suspicion could lead to disbelief of the ad and a rejection of the message. A third effect is that some segments of consumers may be offended by the stereotyping and may publicly criticize the ad or organize movements against the advertiser. A fourth effect is that some segments may compare the models to their own self, leading to feelings of inadequacy and self-destructive behavior.[21]

For example, some critics claim that the incredibly perfect models in many ads lead female teenagers to embark on impossible diet and exercise regimens that harm their bodies. These critics go so far as to assert that the problems of bulimia and anorexia among female teens is partly if not largely due to the models in contemporary ads. On the other hand, scientific evidence suggests that all bulimia and anorexia are psychological problems with roots in family upbringing or even genetics.

In recent years, some advertisers have been more sensitive to these issues, while others have proceeded with the usual stereotypes. Ads for products such as beer, jeans, and perfume fall in the latter group. For example, early in 2003 Miller Lite aired an ad that showed two scantily clad women involved in a mud fight over the taste versus low calories of the brand. While the ad was widely criticized for its poor taste, the company scheduled three sequels to the ad because of its apparent success with the target audience. Beyond the mere number of male and female models is the issue of the roles, postures, and attire of these models. A study suggests that while there is a trend toward more equal presentation among male and female models, the gap may be quite wide.[22]

Age Stereotypes

Age stereotyping has probably been less offensive and more subtle than that based on gender. An extensive study of the appearances of the elderly in magazine ads is quite informative.[23] The study analyzed a sample of 5,195 ads from four issues of each of nine magazines covering distinct topics over a 30-year period (1950-1980). One finding was a steady increase in the appearance of the elderly in ads from 6.8% in 1950 to 11% in 1980 compared with 12% to 16% of the elderly in the population. The increasing trend probably reflects the greater buying power of the elderly and greater consciousness about the need to be age neutral. Another finding was that older persons were generally presented in working situations, mostly in prestigious jobs. This portrayal is not necessarily bad. However, there is a dramatic difference in the casting of endorsers across product category from a low of .7% elderly in cosmetics to a high of 21% elderly in liquor. Research shows that food (e.g., soft drinks), hygiene (shampoo), clothing, and cosmetics ads tend to frequently cast their spokespersons as young and beautiful. A third more dramatic difference is that among elderly spokespersons, males exceeded females 4 to 1.

Thus, advertisers have still to realize that stereotyping in any form is morally repugnant and practically self-defeating. Audiences may be offended by the stereotypes and may reject the messenger, the message, and the product.

Summary

Three theories explain the role of endorsers: source attractiveness, source credibility, and meaning transfer. Each of these theories explains specific contexts and processes in which endorsements are effective. These three theories are complementary. However, the meaning transfer theory is probably the most important because it is often neglected. It suggests that the meaning of the endorsers and the message of the brand needs to be in congruence.

Endorsers can be broadly classified as experts, celebrities, or lay endorsers. The theories provide different rationales for the use of endorsers. They also explain which of the three types of endorsers are most relevant. The meaning transfer theory is most relevant for celebrities. The source credibility theory is most relevant for experts. The source attractiveness theory is most relevant for lay endorsers. An advertiser's selection of either an expert, celebrity, or lay endorser also depends on the characteristics of the brand, message, and especially the target audience for the ad.

Notes

1.   Jensen, Jeff (1993), "Bowe Is Endorsement Heavyweight, Too," *Advertising Age*, June 14.

2.   Dean, Dwane Hal, and Abhijit Biswas (2001), "Third-Party Organization Endorsement of Products: An Advertising Cue Affecting Consumer Prepurchase Evaluation of Goods and Services," *Journal of Advertising*, 30, 4 (Winter), 41-57.

3.   McCracken, Grant (1989), "Who Is a Celebrity Endorser?" *Journal of Consumer Research*, 16 (December), 310-321.

4.   Ibid.

5.   For example, for effectiveness of same sex endorser, see Bochner, Stephen (1994), "The Effectiveness of Same-Sex Versus Opposite-Sex Role Models in Advertisements to Reduce Alcohol Consumption in Teenagers," *Addictive Behaviors*, 19, 1 (January-February), 69-82.

6.   Caballero, Marjorie, James R. Lumpkin, and Charles S. Madden (1989), "Using Physical Attractiveness as an Advertising Tool," *Journal of Advertising Research*, 29, 4.

7.   McCracken, "Who Is a Celebrity Endorser?"

8.   Hsu, Chung-Kue, and Daniella McDonald (2002), "An Examination on Multiple Celebrity Endorsers in Advertising," *Journal of Product and Brand Management Year*, 11, 1, 19; Till, Brian D., and Michael Busler (2000), "The Match-Up Hypothesis: Physical Attractiveness, Expertise, and the Role of Fit on Brand Attitude, Purchase Intent and Brand Beliefs," *Journal of Advertising*, 29, 3 (Fall), 1-15; Kamins, Michael A., and Kamal Gupta (1994), "Congruence Between Spokesperson and Product Type: A Match Up Hypothesis Perspective," *Psychology & Marketing*, 11, 6 (November-December), 569-586.

9.   Daneshvary, Rennae, and R. Keith Schwer (2000), "The Association Endorsement and Consumers' Intention to Purchase," *Journal of Consumer Marketing*, 17, 3, 203-213; Stafford, Marla Royne, Thomas F. Stafford, and Ellen Day (2002), "A Contingency Approach: The Effects of Spokesperson Type and Service Type on Service Advertising Perceptions," *Journal of Advertising*, 31, 2 (Summer), 17-36; Freiden, Jon B. (1982), "An Evaluation of Spokesperson and Vehicle Source Effects in Advertising," *Current Issues and Research in Advertising*, 77-87.

10.   McCracken, "Who Is a Celebrity Endorser?"

11.   Colford, Steven W. (1991), "How to Find the Right Spokesman," *Advertising Age*, October 28, 17.

12.   Kamins and Gupta, "Congruence Between Spokesperson and Product Type."

13.   King, Thomas R. (1985), "More Pros Find Celebrity Ads Unpersuasive," *Wall Street Journal*, July 5, B1.

14.   "It Seemed Like a Good Idea at the Time," *Forbes*, February 28, 1987, 98.

15.   Carolyn Tripp, Thomas D. Jensen, and Les Carlson (1994), "The Effects of Multiple Product Endorsements by Celebrities on Consumers' Attitudes and Intentions," *Journal of Consumer Research*, 20, 4 (March), 535-547.

16.   Ibid.

17.   Lipman, Joanne (1990), "When It's Commercial Time Viewers Prefer Cartoons to Celebrities Any Day," *Wall Street Journal*, B10.

18. Till, Brian D., and Terence A. Shimp (1998), "Endorsers in Advertising: The Case of Negative Celebrity Information," *Journal of Advertising,* 27, 1 (Spring), 67-82.

19. Lipman, Joanne (1992), "Pairing Stars With Sneakers Is Reassessed," *Wall Street Journal,* September 9, B6.

20. Bentley, Tim (2003), "Lolita Behind the Camera: Nature of Fashion Photography With Connections to Nabokov's Lolita," http://www.coh.arizona.edu/inst/eng102-lolita/essays/bentley.html.

21. Richins, Marsha L. (1991), "Social Comparison and the Idealized Images of Advertising," *Journal of Consumer Research,* 18 (June), 71-83.

22. Bellizi, Joseph, and Laura Milner (1991), "Gender Positioning of a Traditionally Male-Dominated Product," *Journal of Advertising Research* (June/July), 72-79.

23. Ursic, Anthony C., Michael L. Ursic, and Virginia L. Ursic (1986), "A Longitudinal Study of the Use of the Elderly in Magazine Advertising," *Journal of Consumer Research,* 13, 1 (June).

Index

About the Author

Gerard J. Tellis holds the Jerry & Nancy Neely Chair in American Enterprise and is Professor of Marketing at the Marshall School of Business, the University of Southern California, Los Angeles. He has also served as Distinguished Visiting Professor at Erasmus University Rotterdam, the Netherlands; Visiting Professor of Marketing, Strategy and Innovation at the Judge Institute of Management, Cambridge University, United Kingdom; and Visiting Fellow of Sidney Sussex College, Cambridge University, United Kingdom. He has a Ph.D. in business administration from the University of Michigan, Ann Arbor. Previously, he worked as a Sales Development Manager for Johnson & Johnson.

Dr. Tellis specializes in advertising, promotion, new product growth, market entry, and technological innovation. He has published more than 50 articles and books. His articles have appeared in leading scholarly journals, including the *Journal of Marketing Research, Journal of Marketing, Marketing Science, Journal of Advertising Research, Strategic Management Journal,* and *Sloan Management Review* and have won numerous awards, including four of the most prestigious awards in the field of marketing: the Harold D. Maynard (twice), William F. Odell, and Frank M. Bass awards, and the Berry–American Marketing Association Book Prize.

His latest book, *Will and Vision: How Latecomers Grow to Dominate Markets* (coauthored with Peter Golder), refutes the common belief in first-mover advantages and explains the real causes of enduring market leadership. The book was cited as one of the top 10 books in business by the *Harvard Business Review* and won the Berry–AMA Award for the best book in marketing. His book on advertising and sales promotion strategy has been translated into three languages. He has been on the editorial review boards of the *Journal of Marketing Research, Journal of Marketing,* and *Marketing Science* for several years.